Written by Kay Cooke

Edited by Jane Pikett

All rights reserved 2022 ©Happy Brain Co Ltd

Society of NLP™, DHE®, NHR®, Bandler®, Persuasion Engineering®, belong to John La Valle.

No part of this book may be used or reproduced by any means, graphic, electronic, or mechanical, including photocopying, recording, taping or by any information storage retrieval system without the written permission of the author except in the case of brief quotations embodied in critical articles and reviews. The content of this book is entertaining and educational and is not intended to be a source of advice and should not be construed as, nor replace, medical or psychiatric advice. The publisher and author provide this book and its contents on an "as is" basis and make no representations or warranties of any kind with respect to this book or its contents. In addition, the publisher and the author assume no responsibility for errors, inaccuracies, omissions, or any other inconsistencies herein and hereby disclaim any liability to any party for any loss, damage, or disruption caused by errors or omissions, whether such errors or omissions result from negligence, accident, or any other cause.

ISBN: 978-1-7399720-6-6

the happy brain co.

www.thehappybrainco.com

INSPIRATIONS
for thriving
through chaos

Dr Richard Bandler, Alexander Millar, Kathleen La Valle
Joy A Thorne, Dr Mark Chambers, Louie B Free
John La Valle, Tracey Hutchinson, Kate Benson
Chris Cummins, Heiko Wenig

Inspiring conversations
with **Kay Cooke**

Dedication

When I was a little girl, I wanted to be wise like my daddy, who always seemed to know everything about everything.
But as I grew up, I discovered that in fact he didn't know everything, because as I later realised, his knowledge, understanding and perspectives expanded through time.
His endless curiosity and fascination for how life works, and his ability to perceive that from so many perspectives, taught me to constantly seek great wisdoms that reveal themselves through the process of lifelong learning. Dad, you are a constant inspiration!

ABOUT THIS BOOK

This book chronicles a series of conversations recorded during the Covid pandemic between coach, therapist and NLP trainer Kay Cooke and inspirational people from around the world, with NLP (Neuro Linguistic Programming) being the common thread.

As the pandemic spread, Kay set out to have public conversations with people whose perspectives might inspire in others a focus on thrive rather than the feelings of survival many people felt. She called the series *Live Thrive* and the conversations documented here, which span two years, are as thought-provoking now as they were when they were recorded.

Each chapter brings a slightly different outlook and approach, yet they all share powerful insights into how we can adopt a thrive mindset in the face of challenge now and in future, providing a blueprint for resilience we can all learn from.

CONTENTS

Preface   13

INTERVIEWS

1   DR RICHARD BANDLER   14-29

The great thinker, philosopher, teacher and co-founder of Neuro Linguistic Programming (NLP) shares his wisdoms for resilience

2   ALEXANDER MILLAR   30-53

This internationally renowned artist shares his personal journey and the enlightened thinking which underpins his life philosophy

3   KATHLEEN LA VALLE   54-89

A world-renowned NLP teacher and coach, Kathleen inspires us to venture beyond our limitations through our innate creativity

4   JOY A THORNE   90-99

The New Forest's wise woman reveals her nature-based approach to spirituality and human development

5   DR MARK CHAMBERS   100-131

Dr Mark Chambers' innovative work as a generative coach inspires this chat about the natural programming we can all find within

| **6** | **LOUIE B FREE** | 132-149 |

US radio presenter Louie reveals his driving passion to share the psychologies of wellbeing with the world

| **7** | **JOHN LA VALLE** | 150-175 |

The President of the Society of NLP™ discusses the need to adapt and grow new behaviours in a fast-changing world

| **8** | **TRACEY HUTCHINSON** | 176-195 |

A people development specialist, Tracey shares her strategies for bringing calm into contemporary mind matters

| **9** | **KATE BENSON** | 196-215 |

A leading educator, Kate shares her passion for helping the next generation flourish and her support for struggling familes

| **10** | **CHRIS CUMMINS** | 216-229 |

The leader of a global business, Chris discusses the principles that underpin his company's approach to wellbeing

| **11** | **HEIKO WENIG** | 230-253 |

A leading teacher of energy, consciousness and healing, Heiko shares his views on flourishing within this changing world

Afterword   254-255

PREFACE

Very often when I'm in conversation with certain people, a nugget of inspiration will dance through my awareness. When I'm fast enough, I can catch it in my notebook or on phone notes. Sometimes a conversation replays in my mind, as if it is asking to be explored and its value revealed. Words have great power, and conversations can inspire new trains of thought and consolidate those that were previously unexplored or untethered, which can bring healing to inner troubles.

As the world went into lockdown in 2020, my first response was to have public conversations with people whose perspectives might inspire in others a focus on thrive rather than survive. I called the series *Live Thrive* and it reflected a moment of our times where the world descended into chaos. Yet so many of these wisdoms are as valid today, and will be tomorrow, as they were yesterday. And as that awareness reverberated through the recesses of my mind, I knew this book was forming.

I hope you'll be inspired. Maybe by the whole book, a specific chapter, or certain words or phrases. Perhaps you'll enjoy connecting to new levels of consciousness that are developing in these times. I hope that within this smorgasbord of interviews, there is inspiration for everyone.

Kay Cooke
February 2022

Chapter one: Dr Richard Bandler

DR RICHARD BANDLER

Dr Richard Bandler is one of my all time favourite teachers of conscious thinking, having continually developed human change technologies for the past 50 years. He is the co-founder of Neuro Linguistic Programming (NLP) and I've been a student of his for almost 20 years, immersed in his technologies that include Licensed Practitioner and Master Practitioner of NLP™, Neuro Hypnotic Repatterning®, Design Human Engineering®, Persuasion Engineering®, Personal Enhancement™, Charisma Enhancement®, Hypnosis, and many more. In April 2020, just as the world was reeling from being locked down due to Covid-19, Richard kindly agreed to share some of his wisdoms for resilience.

Chapter one: Dr Richard Bandler

Kay: Richard, while we could talk about NLP in general today, what people are asking for and desperately need right now when much of the world is in lockdown, is resilience. So first of all, I wonder if you might be able to share some of your thoughts about the topic of resilience.

Richard: Well, in a nutshell, resilience is your ability to rebound from difficulty. And on planet Earth, I can guarantee things will go wrong. You know, people die, people have divorces, businesses collapse. I prefer not to think of this current period as a pandemic lockdown, but as the 'grand pause'.

We've all had to take this grand pause in our life; the question is, how do you look at it? Because you know, a lot of the people I've talked to are sitting around fantasising about how bad it can be and about getting the virus, and I think that's bad planning. I think that if you get the virus, you should be thinking about getting over it. And if you don't, you should be thinking about how to avoid it and, importantly, how to spend the extra time you have now, during this pause.

I got an email from the local symphony here in Dallas. They said that during the grand pause, they were going to broadcast on a radio station and rehearse even more special pieces of music. And they went down a list of things they were going to do to become a better orchestra.

I think all of us can look at this grand pause as an opportunity; one, to catch up on things, and two, to take the opportunity to plan how we're going to come back ferociously. And you see, if you're going to make pictures in your head, you might as well make ones where you succeed, because your brain is going to do whatever it is you think about. That's because once you start thinking about things, your neurology lines up to follow.

Chapter one: Dr Richard Bandler

Successful athletes don't sit around and imagine failing unless they go into a slump. And every time I work with an athlete who's done really well for a while and then starts doing poorly, they start asking questions like, "What if this slump never ends?" To which I'm going to say, "Well everything ends, you know?" Take World War 2; people thought it would never end, but they did keep on thinking about how to end it, and that's what got it over with.

When you look at yourself in your mind and see yourself having problems, resilience is built out of changing that picture – literally putting a better picture in its place. The people who survived concentration camps in the war didn't survive by giving up. The people who did that faded away and died. Take the people I talked to when I wrote my book *The Secrets of Being Happy*. There's medical research about how being happy allows you to have a stronger immune system. That's because it's good for you to be a happy person. But happy isn't like 'la, la, la la...' Happy is actually when people feel they have a purpose.

Small business owners are being hit very hard right now. They have to start thinking about how they're going to use this time to be prepared to come back ferociously. When this is over, people aren't going to be jumping into restaurants and running out to have their nails done, because they're going to be cautious, so those businesses are going to have to entice them. They're going to have to make sure their place of business is safe.

When you're a resilient person, when you get hit over the head with the worst of everything your response is to become more determined. Whenever I interviewed very successful people early in my career, I would ask them, "What made you, when you were poor with few resources, determined to make your business so successful?" Three quarters of them would stop and think about the question and their expression would change, they'd place their

Chapter one: Dr Richard Bandler

fingers on the two points right below the eye, and then start to talk. So I started talking to my clients who were not so determined and got them to focus on those two points, the ones right below the eye. I'd say, "If you just concentrate in your mind and think about it, you let your focus and your attention go to your ears and then just go across to here and focus, you'll discover you just feel more determined."

I don't know why that's the case. It's probably some connection between the neurons in your brain and your eyes, and states of consciousness. I'm sure that neurologically, we'll figure it out someday. And in the meanwhile, once you start to feel even a little determined, you can start to make pictures of yourself being more determined. And the more determined you are, the more resilient you will be.

"When you look at yourself in your mind and see yourself having problems, resilience is built out of changing the picture"

I guarantee all of us are going to take a hit through the current situation. I've been home for three weeks; they've cancelled almost everything I was supposed to be doing this year. But I'm not thinking about going under, I'm thinking about how I'm going to make it through and how I'm going to come back twice as strong. And that's what everybody should be doing.

The other thing is that this grand pause is a perfect opportunity to be determined to catch up on the things you haven't caught up on, like cleaning that closet you haven't cleaned. That is, to stay

Chapter one: Dr Richard Bandler

in the mode of being busy, of having a purpose. Don't just let this time wear you down, because then you won't be resilient.

When people have a purpose, they're always happier. So make a list of all the things you've been meaning to do. A lot of people want to start painting, drawing, playing music, going back to learning the guitar. This is a perfect opportunity, because probably when you started those things, the internet wasn't as full of lessons as it is now.

My grandson came to visit me. He came in my studio, he looked at my guitar and he said, "I'm learning to play the guitar." And I said, "Would you like a lesson?" And he said, "Na, there are thousands on YouTube that are better than you are." And he got on my computer and showed me great musicians giving lessons. And I thought well, that's great; I wish that had been around when I was young. Your ability to learn new things is endless now, given the internet. So now, if you place those bad pictures in your head, shut them down, and instead make pictures of spending your time wisely, you will become more resilient.

Kay: Richard, you were talking about using this grand pause as a gap that we can use. We can transform, we have an opportunity to create or alchemise something wonderful from this experience.

I see many people who have the sense of purpose you've identified as being really important, but they make their purpose survival, rather than thriving. And much of my work seems to be about catching them in their states of stress and transforming that stress towards the possibilities of thriving. Do you think some people are born with a natural propensity to want to focus on survival rather than the opportunities for thriving? Or do you think a thrive focus is something people acquire over time and habituate?

Chapter one: Dr Richard Bandler

Richard: Well, I don't think it's genetic. They say survival is the strongest instinct, but many years ago, Virginia Satir, who was one of my teachers, asked me what I thought the strongest instinct in human beings was, and like a robot, I said survival. And she said no, people will kill themselves rather than face the unknown. You know, like the people who are in a marriage for 30 years, then one leaves and the other goes and hangs themself in the closet?

I lived in San Francisco for many years, and every year there'd be 10 or 15 people who would jump off the Golden Gate Bridge; that's not survival being the strongest instinct. I think the strongest instinct in human beings is to make things familiar. It's what your brain is designed to do.

Being in survival mode can be about self-esteem, and it can be about poverty. Right now, people are trying to out-buy each other in toilet paper. It's hysterical; go to the supermarket and there are empty shelves where it used to be. They've put out a sign – 'one pack per customer' – like you need to tell somebody that! I mean, good God, how long do they think this is going to go on that they need 500 rolls of toilet paper to survive it? That's not a very optimistic point of view. For some people, it's become something they can grasp: "If I have enough toilet paper, I'll make it through."

But making it through isn't enough. You want to make it through gloriously. And the way to do that is to spend the currency of living intelligently. The currency of living is not money. Contrary to what many people believe, the currency of living is how you spend each moment, and you don't know how many moments you're going to get in your life. And if you don't plan how you're going to spend those moments, you won't spend them wisely.

It's like money. In the US, we have a financial guy on the radio all the time who helps people get out of debt, and there are so

Chapter one: Dr Richard Bandler

many people in debt. He wrote a book, *Living Debt Free*, which tells you how to get down your credit card debt and mortgage, so you get to the point where you don't owe anybody anything.

He says the big thing for the next decade isn't having a fancy car, it's being debt-free. And certainly, given Uber, you don't need a car, especially if you live in a city.

But how you plan and spend the moments of your life is the most important thing. And now we know the grand pause is going to last for a while, make a big plan so you have more to do than you have time to spend. That includes spending time with your family, your kids. There will be a point where you'll have had enough and want a break, whether it's going in the other room or driving very slowly to the supermarket. Because it's not what you do with your time, it's the quality of how you spend it. And if you spend it wisely, you live wisely.

> *"People confuse remembering with thinking. When they say they can't do something, they're only remembering that they haven't. They're not thinking that they can and trying it in a new way"*

Kay: Do you think people will become more aware of the things that really matter to them now? Will there be a shift in people's values?

Chapter one: Dr Richard Bandler

Richard: I think people who spend their time wisely will appreciate it. I think the more people we can get to do that, the better. Most of the people that I've modelled who were successful at things asked certain good questions. And the people that come in as clients, whether they're rich or poor, all ask the same bad questions: "What if this bad time never ends?" "What if I get so far in debt, I can never get out?"

These kind of loaded questions get you to think bad thoughts, make bad pictures, talk to yourself in a bad tonality and make bad feelings. And it all feeds on itself. Grand pause or not, I've been working; we never seem to run out of people who know how to undermine the quality of their own lives, and it's all done with bad planning.

Part of the reason I wrote the book *Thinking on Purpose* was because over all the years I've worked with people, the one thing I can count on is that most of them confuse remembering with thinking. So when they say they think they can't do something, they're only remembering that they haven't. They're not thinking that they can and then trying it in a new way.

My great uncle became a millionaire three times and got completely wiped out three times, not because of something he did, but because of external forces. One was the unions destroyed his business. He had the fourth largest trucking company in the northeast and the unions fire-bombed his trucks because he wouldn't join the union; his employees didn't want to because he paid them more than the union said. And eventually they took the company away from him. He drove away and he had nothing but a broken-down old car. And when he got to New York, the car broke. He rolled into a gas station and the guy said he couldn't fix it until the weekend because he couldn't close the station to go buy parts. So my uncle asked him how many cars he needed parts for, then

Chapter one: Dr Richard Bandler

went and bought the parts at a discount and sold them back to the guy for a profit. Then he built up a big business out of it.

He told me that when a business fails, then you have to be able to listen quietly inside, because there's this amazing thing that happens. You know, all the people who are talking and whining now aren't listening and watching. And the people who listen and watch will find something to do, an opportunity to learn.

I went into a diner once when I was fairly young, I think probably in my late teens or early 20s. There were two customers; one was complaining about how he didn't make enough money blah, blah, and the other was complaining about all the rich people who got everything too easy. I looked down on the floor between the two of them and there was a $50 bill on the floor, crumpled up underneath the stool. I got up, bent over and picked up the bill. Then I looked towards the guy to the right of me and there was a quarter, so I picked that up too. And then I looked the other way and there was a dollar three or four bar stools down, so I went and picked that up. So while they're busy whining, there's money sitting on the floor. And I always remember that, because when you quiet yourself on the inside, you look for opportunity in every instance.

Now, if you listen to the news, they're always trying to make things worse to make it more dramatic. They say, "But what if…? What if it gets worse? And why did the people in charge do this? And why didn't they know everything ahead of time? And they coulda, woulda, shoulda…"

And, as I'm fond of telling my students, you know you can shit in one hand and wish in the other and one of them will stick. And if you smack yourself in the face, you'll know which one. It's not about wishing; it's about noticing, it's about planning. And if you make good plans in your mind when the moment is right, you will find it.

Kay: I was talking to an NLP colleague the other day, who shared his experience of flying back into the UK from Orlando in late March 2020. Instantly, the airport was very different, and he was the only customer on the taxi rank as the UK was locking down. He runs a big training company, and his brain was saying, "Oh no, I'm losing everything. All my training work is being cancelled and my customers are postponing everything." And very quickly, he reorganised it all and said, "Right, what do I need to do now? I have to do something different." And he started to think about online training programmes and how to capitalise on the new opportunities presenting themselves.

When you talk about thinking on purpose – which is such an important statement for all of us in our work – remembering how to behave versus deciding how to behave, to think and then feel and then do, requires a bit of a skill and wisdom, I feel.

Richard: Well, it requires practice, and it requires that you do it on purpose. And sometimes when you do things on purpose, they don't feel natural until you do them for a while. I found that out learning to play the piano. There's nothing natural about what you do when you learn to play the piano. It comes easier to some

> *"All the people who are talking and whining now aren't listening and watching. And the people who listen and watch will find something to do, an opportunity to learn"*

Chapter one: Dr Richard Bandler

people than others of course, and I don't know if that's genetics or neurology or whatever, but even the best musicians I've ever met, when they learn something new, it feels awkward. Then you do it enough times, you sleep a few times, and you wake up, and suddenly it becomes second nature. And thinking on purpose should become second nature to everyone, because this is not the only grand pause, or little pause that life is going to give you.

There's going to be stuff that happens in your life that's going to disrupt things. Bad things will happen, and the question is, what do you do? Every relationship is going to end in tragedy because somebody is going to die first. And if it becomes the end of the world, well… I've had clients come to me from a psychiatrist, and they've been grieving for over 30 years over the loss of someone, and they're still dressed in black. When they come to me, I have to get them to stop remembering the loss and making it the biggest picture in their head. Because you know, you can re-live any bad memory as many times as you want, and that doesn't make it a good plan. And I've found that if you just shrink those pictures down to the size of a quarter and blink them black and white, they don't come up so much.

That's not a psychological trick. It's a neurological trick. My book is filled with all kinds of things like that, to make it easier for people to think. Because when you change the way you think, it changes the way you feel and therefore it changes what you're capable of doing. And when you get used to doing it, it becomes more automatic. That's why it doesn't surprise me that one of my students in Florida went home and went, "oh, my God, everything is falling apart," and then answered the question, "okay what can I do about it now, and how can I do better in the future?"

I was talking about Dave Ramsey earlier – that's the financial guru. Not only does he get people out of debt, he also tells them they need an emergency fund. And I don't care who you are, you need a back-up fund. You know, the older you get, the more you need to have a back-up fund. One time, my mother called me on the phone, and she said, "I had everything under control in my life, and my septic tank flooded, and now I'm going to have to re-mortgage my house."

So I asked her, "Over the years, didn't you put some money in the bank?" I mean, all she had to do was take a part of her monthly income and stick it in the bank, and 30 years later she would have had a pile for an emergency fund. But a lot of people don't plan on the fact that things are going to go wrong. And things will, so you either have to hawk what you have, or you have to have planned. This is a good time for people to notice what they didn't do so that they plan to do it in the future.

You remember when some people invested in the stock market too heavily and took a big hit? The problem when you take a hit in the stock market, like in 2008, is that if you have $1,000-worth of stock and it drops in half because the stock market goes down, then you have half that much to invest to get back. And if the stock market goes right back up to where it was, you're still only going to have 70% of what you had. So it's always a good idea to have backup money that you can use to survive difficult times.

For this grand pause, a lot of people weren't prepared. They didn't even have back-up toilet paper, for heaven's sake. There are certain supplies you should keep around. You know, I'm not a survivalist, but I keep a little survivalist food around, just in case, because you never know.

I don't know at what point we'll ever be truly safe from this virus. I'm over 70, so I'm judged to be very vulnerable, but there was a guy in his 90s who got it and survived. So which guy are you going to be? The guy who gives in or the guy who survives? To me, you

Chapter one: Dr Richard Bandler

should always plan strongly. And you know, if you can imagine yourself getting sick, you can imagine yourself getting well quickly. Even better to build a barrier around yourself and decide you're not going to be one of the ones that gets it. And if you do, then heal yourself as quickly as possible and start thinking about what you're going to do on the other side of the grand pause.

Kay: That's great advice. I remember when we were in Orlando a month or so ago, you emphasised to us the importance of staying in good shape neurologically with really good brain-body chemistry, so that our immune systems had the best possible chance of being supported.

Richard: That's right. The question about how we spend our time, and the time you spend in your mind, is the most important of all. Remember when you asked me earlier, do I think resilience is genetic or do I think it's learned? I think it's about the beliefs we have built, both growing up and later in life. The question of whether somebody is a pessimist or an optimist has never been the question. People say, "Are you a half glass half full or glass half empty person?" And I say, "Where are the rest of the glasses?"

This time is a good opportunity to go inside and start cleaning up the pictures and voices in your head. The one thing that belongs

> *"If you change the way you think, it will change the way you feel, and therefore it will change what you're capable of doing"*

Chapter one: Dr Richard Bandler

to you is the interior of your mind. And if you change the way you think, it will change the way you feel, and therefore it will change what you're capable of doing.

It's whenever you have a belief that limits your choice and your ability to feel good, like those people who tell me they can't learn a musical instrument. Every time they pick it up and feel bad and make a sound that doesn't sound right, they feel bad. If they change the way they feel and just start making sounds, start following instructions on YouTube, pretty soon they're going to be able to do it. Every mistake, everything that doesn't work, should make you more determined to do it another way.

So the big lesson to take away from this conversation is determination. You know, staying focused on the future, good hygiene in the way that we organise our thoughts, and resilience fuelled by determination. And if the more things don't go your way the more determined you get, eventually you will succeed – as long as you don't keep making the same mistakes. And the biggest mistake you can make is to go inside yourself and think something should have worked when it didn't.

The history of psychiatry and psychotherapy, when I started, was a record of all the schools of psychotherapy doing the same thing. And when clients didn't change, it was blamed on them. When something didn't work for me with a client, I never did it again with that person. I looked at every client case history as a list of things that wouldn't work rather than a description of the patient. And when I did that, I started finding out what would work.

Over 50 years, I was successful where many other people had failed. That was only because I refused to do things that didn't work and instead tried anything else. I took things out of science fiction, I took things from neurology, I tried all kinds of things. You know, I had people take their mental pictures and just turn them

Chapter one: Dr Richard Bandler

around and see what was on the other side; whatever it took to get somebody to feel different so that they could act differently in the world. The more they acted differently, the more they thought differently, the better they felt.

The road to success starts in changing the way you think. You change the way you think, it changes how you feel, therefore it changes what you can do. So remembering is great when you're remembering something that works. But when you're remembering something that just makes you feel bad because it didn't work, stop thinking about it and think about something else.

Kay: This is amazing wisdom, and you make it sound so simple.

Richard: Well, as you know, it is simple. The hard part is starting to do it. And you know, most people think the same way because they've always thought that way. I can't tell you how many times I've said to a client, "You know you're terrified all the time; what are you thinking about?" And they reply, "Well, I've got this great big picture of this horrible thing happening." And when I look at them and I say, "Has it ever occurred to you to just not make this picture?" a lot of them look at me and say they didn't know consciously they were doing it. And I say, "Well now that you do, let's take that picture and just white it out suddenly or shrink it down to the size of a nickel, fade to black and white. Turn it upside down or put circus music with it, and you know, once you start doing even random things, you know silliness is a lot better than suffering."

You know we always say, "You're going to look back and laugh"? My policy is, why wait?

Kay: Absolutely. At the moment, some of us NLP trainers are looking at beginning to offer small chunks of NLP training online.

Richard: You can train people to think better and make changes in themselves, and you can train people to help their clients. Certainly, people are learning that changing the way you think has a lot of dimensions to it. It goes on in business, it goes on in your personal life. It goes on in habits. You can get better at piano if you know how to visualise the keyboard in your mind, imagine what chords look like and put your fingers on them. There's a tremendous amount of training that could be done online with NLP.

Kay: And that's all part of the big adventure. It's a very exciting time for us.

Richard: We're all looking forward. The world will open up at different times and different places; we don't want to do it too fast, and we don't want to do it too slow. It's like everything else in life; it has to have its own perfect rhythm. In the meanwhile, we'll all find alternative ways of connecting with the people of the planet.

www.richardbandler.com

ALEXANDER MILLAR

Alexander Millar is an internationally known artist and a friend of more than 20 years. This conversation took place in mid-2020, in the midst of a UK-wide lockdown, and in it we chart something of Alexander's story from window cleaner to famous artist, renowned for his signature paintings of 'gadgies' (working-class men) which strike a chord with people worldwide, and his more recent foray into owning and running his own galleries, both in the UK and in the US, where New York City has a particular pull on his heart.

Chapter two: Alexander Millar

Alexander: I fondly remember coming to the art gallery you had in the 2000s probably every day, throwing my woes at your feet, trying to get some advice about art, then talking life and the universe and everything at the time. It was great fun...

Kay: So what's been happening for you since those heady days of rising to great stardom as an international artist?

Alexander: So much. I was tied to a contract with a big art publisher, which was a double-edged sword. Yes, it was good because I had regular sales and a steady income, but I was on a treadmill, having to churn out paintings non-stop.

When you start as an artist, you'll accept any contract just to get going. And that's not the best thing, because once you're trapped in that contract and things take off, you're stuck with your little piece of the pie. And when you become popular, you expect the piece of the pie to get bigger. And the men in suits are businessmen, not artists, so they keep your piece of the pie quite small, and they take the profits. So I couldn't wait to get out of that contract, and I eventually did, but it took me 10 years.

Since then, I've been self-publishing and self-promoting, and I've discovered that you need the right people around you when you go out on your own. So I found a guy I used to work with under one of the old contracts. I told him I needed somebody to take care of the business side because it's all left-hemisphere mentally, whereas I'm all unicorns and rainbows. From there we managed to launch our first Alexander Miller Fine Art Gallery in Glasgow, and it's been great since.

Then we got an opportunity to do a show for the New York Fire Department Museum, which led to renting a place in Soho in New York. The guy who owned it fell in love with the work and

Chapter two: Alexander Millar

said it would sell really well midtown, where he had a space near the Flatiron Building. I asked where that was and he said, "Oh, it's on Fifth Avenue." And I thought, hang on, I've gone from being a window cleaner to being an artist with a Fifth Avenue art gallery!

Then we got the opportunity to open a place in Newcastle-upon-Tyne, England, where I live. So it's been quite a whirlwind. And that's what life should be – full of adventure. It's a journey of ups and downs and bends and turns, but there should always be wee lay-bys where you can stop and just see where you are in life. Always look out for the lay-bys.

> *"Life kind of carries you like a gentle breeze; it floats you along to where you're meant to be…"*

Kay: Always look out for the lay-bys – what a great piece of advice for the world. So there's a huge amount in there about creativity and resilience and going with the flow and so on. And when I first met you, you were still doing a bit of window cleaning, weren't you?

Alexander: I was. I always laugh because when it was raining I was painting, and when it was clear I was window cleaning. A lot of people come up to that cliff edge where there's an opportunity, but it's a scary opportunity, like you can't see the bottom because you just see a dark hole. And a lot of people don't jump. When I was going through my dark night of the soul, my unconscious pushed me over that edge. It was the scariest thing in the world to do, but the most beneficial, most exciting thing I've ever done, and

Chapter two: Alexander Millar

I would encourage anybody that if and when you come to that cliff edge, just bite the bullet and jump and see where life takes you.

I've found that the more you surrender yourself to life and stop kicking and pushing and shoving and forcing, life kind of carries you. It's like a gentle breeze; it floats you along and it'll take you where you're meant to be. So often we think we should be here, when really we should be over there. Once you surrender yourself to life, it will take you to the destination you're meant to be.

Kay: You're talking about the flow state we often discuss, and I remember in those early days of what you've just called the dark night of the soul, you didn't jump into the dark hole. I remember you had, whether you were conscious of it or not, a vision of your future. You had a vision of yourself as a successful artist of global recognition, and I remember you talking about visualising yourself going to America, for example. And there was something else guiding you there, whether you call that inner wisdom or whatever, it doesn't really matter where it comes from, but you weren't just jumping blindly. You had vision about what the future might be like.

Alexander: That's right. Until you understand how the unconscious mind works, you only have desires and wants and needs, but I would encourage people to understand life a bit more, because when you go to school, you get taught mathematics and to read and write, etc. I said this to my daughter the other day, because she's homeschooling her kids, and I said, "Stop schooling them, they're six and four, so let them play and forget about school."

You'll only take less than 10% what you learned at school into modern adult life, and it's when you get into adulthood that you

Chapter two: Alexander Millar

have to understand life's secrets. And really, you have to understand those secrets, because there are secrets in life; there are secrets nobody wants you to know, and school, university, the education system won't teach you those things.

So I had the desire to be a world-famous artist and hadn't a clue how it was going to happen. But as we know, if you visualise, thoughts become things. So when I was in that dark night of the soul, I kept that at the forefront of my imagination.

You have to visualise and keep that at the forefront, and that makes jumping off that cliff a little easier, even though you can't see what's at the bottom, because you know there's a safety net. When you visualise, when you imagine it's already happened, it will happen. You have to go up to the cliff and actually jump in; force yourself over the cliff and jump.

I knew a lot of people who were on antidepressants. I had depression as well, and the pills will help you to a point and your unconscious will push you up to the cliff edge and you think, "Oh my God, no," because it's a scary place to be. So you start going to the doctor and you're popping the pills, and your mind will retreat from the cliff. And then you ease off the pills and your unconscious goes, "Right okay, no pressure," and again, you head back up there. And it's a vicious cycle. People seem to go up to the cliff edge, take the pills, retreat and so on for years and years. People get into that cycle and hold their life up because they're on this treadmill. Yet it was more beneficial for me, even though it was a scary thing, to come up to the edge and jump off and see where life takes you.

There was a video of Will Smith talking about his first skydive and he said it was like coming up to the cliff edge. Standing at the doorway of the plane, ready to jump, his heart was pounding, yet when he jumped and got to the ground, he wanted to do it again

Chapter two: Alexander Millar

because it was the most exciting and invigorating and thrilling thing to do. But you have to give yourself that little bit of faith and confidence that life will support you. Because there is a way for people out of a situation or to a destination because life will always find a way for you. There are the little steps to take that will help you to get where you need and want to be.

Kay: Many people will recognise that what you're talking about is the clarity of a well-formed outcome. So you take yourself forward in life as if it has happened or is happening, with that full sensory experience. I think a lot of people talk about that as manifestation. And of course it is – you're creating the future you; you're the architect and designer of your own life, something you seem to have done so well.

Talking of well-formed outcomes, you were the person who encouraged me to do my first NLP Practitioner course, and it's thanks to you that I embarked on my journey to discover how my mind works and have gone on to have a career in helping other people to help themselves.

Alexander: That's great. It's a great journey to be on, and the thing that helped me when I used to come and visit you at the gallery was being able to talk to you.

You know, I believe that whatever people face in life, if you've got a listening ear, that's more important than anything. I remember I would say the same thing over and over again, and the repetition was like I was wanting reassurance for the journey that I was embarking on.

Talking like that is so important, and you know when the listener guides you in the right direction because you feel it rather than just hearing what they say. You might not understand it, but you feel it

Chapter two: Alexander Millar

in your stomach, you feel that it's right. And that's where it makes sense. That gut feeling. If it makes sense there, go with it.

Kay: Yes, one of the essential core needs of human beings is to have somebody who can listen unconditionally. And it's not necessarily about giving advice; it's about just being present. I volunteer as a Samaritan and that's largely what we do. We're just present with that person completely and utterly, and we're just listening. And it serves a very important function somewhere in the alignment of conscious and unconscious.

Something that has stayed with me all these years as I've grown to understand the power of the unconscious mind through the Bandler® Technologies, something that I was greatly aware of when I owned the art gallery, was watching people's unconscious responses to what they were seeing, what they were experiencing as they viewed the artwork.

That's how I knew your work was going to take off. In those early days, I would have to decide which pieces I would take in, and I found the work that followed all the academic rules for creating art might be perfect, but it didn't get an emotional response from people. And your work got huge emotional responses. I always link that, in NLP terms, to the Milton Model – the ambiguity, what's left out, the suggestion. Everybody could look at one of your gadgies and think, "Oh that's just like my uncle. It's just like my father. It's just like my grandfather. Oh, that's just like so-and-so..." People could fill in the gaps and make the work personal to them, even though it was immensely personal to you, because there was something that was resonating with other people's emotional selves.

Alexander: As you say, it's what isn't there, what's left out, that appeals to people. Most of the figures I paint are viewed from the

Chapter two: Alexander Millar

back, so there are no faces. I learned from an early point in my career that it's the ambiguity of the thing that touches people.

I came across this by accident. I used to have figures in the background of a street scene, say. Some were side views, some were front views. I didn't have models, so I used to go into Newcastle city centre, to places where these old men congregated, and they'd see me sneak up with my camera and go, "Here's that guy back again," and they'd run off and I would chase them with my camera. So all my reference work was guys walking away, and that tied in with what was going on with my father. He was dying at the time, so in a way it made sense unconsciously to me; he was going away from me. So all my work eventually became these old men walking away.

"One of the essential core needs of human beings is to have somebody who can listen unconditionally… just being present"

Then one day I was doing a painting and I had a big pile of white paint left on my mixing pallet, and I thought (typical Scotsman…), I'm not going to let this go to waste. So I painted out the background and suddenly this figure just went 'ta-dah!' and jumped out of the canvas. And I thought, "Oh, my goodness, the more I was taking away from the picture the more it was making sense to me." And that's how the gadgie figures were born.

It made sense when you mentioned people's reaction to them,

Chapter two: Alexander Millar

because there were countless times people would stand and cry in front of them, tears pouring down their faces. I used to put my arm around them and joke, "Are my paintings that bad?" And they'd say, "Oh no, it reminds me of my father, my grandfather, it reminds me of this or that." And so it was that the more I took out of the paintings, the more people were free emotionally to attach themselves to them.

Kay: I remember going from selling a painting of yours, this is 20 years ago, for something like £350, and then £3,500, and then £35,000. It was add a nought, add a nought, add a nought. It was phenomenal.

Alexander: It's funny, because I had a painting above my fireplace at home for years, a very dark scene of a guy looking at the stars, and the number of people who said it resonated. It meant a lot to me because that's exactly how I felt when I came out that dark night. I was like, "Oh my God, I've come through."

I was born and raised a Jehovah's Witness. It was very highly controlled, and life was very black and white. So my life was very structured, very controlling, with five meetings a week, going from door to door, no time to sit and actually think, "Well hang on, who am I?"

When my dad died, I went into a tailspin. I left the religion, I left my community, and it was a very uncomfortable place to be. But that reflected itself in the work and that painting was the moment I knew I had come through, when I realised, "Oh my God, I can breathe," and everything became multi-coloured. It was almost like a colour-blind person could see colour for the first time. I didn't realise the world was like this. I was always told the world was a terrible, horrible place, and to keep away from it. And I was like,

Chapter two: Alexander Millar

"Wow, this is amazing!" So that painting meant a lot to me and I had it for about six years above my fireplace. Then I got an email from a guy in Aberdeen. He'd seen it and been moved by it, and said he wanted to buy it. And to put him off I said, "Well, you'll have to pay me £100,000," and he said, "Okay, send me your bank details." And I was like, "Oh, I'm going to have to let it go." So that was my first £100,000 painting. And when you get to that level, it opens another door, and I've sold more expensive ones since then.

Another thing – never limit yourself to think, "This is my station in life. This is my level." I remember an interview with David Bowie. He said, "If you're a creative type, you should always get to a point where you're up to here in the water and your feet are just at that point where you kind of touch the bottom." And he said that's where the inspiration, the magic, happens. When you get just out of your depth – the uncomfortable bit – that's when you do your best work.

And that's very true; if you get to push the barriers, push the envelope, don't draw a line in the sand – go as far as you can and see where life takes you. Don't put limits on yourself. Watch for doors to open, because as soon as one door opens, there are more. And I found that out way back. Letting go is very powerful.

When you're young and in education, you're taught that if it

"That was the moment I knew I had come through and realised, 'Oh my God, I can breathe' and everything became multi-coloured"

Chapter two: Alexander Millar

doesn't work, if it doesn't move, you should push. The teacher said, you must push harder, try harder. But especially for a right-hemisphere creative type, it's the worst thing to do. Creative types have to stare out of the window. They get the inspiration out there rather than sitting in front of a book. But the education system doesn't recognise that.

I've found that letting go of stuff, not trying to push it, allows life and opportunity to come to you. It's like a relationship. The more you go, "Don't leave me alone, I can't live without you, I need you," the other person will say, "Go away." But the minute you go, "I love you. You can be in my life. You go your way, whatever. I'm not going to stop you. I just want to love you. I'm not going to hold you," the person will love you forever. Life's like that. Don't try to force it; just let go and those doors will open for you.

Kay: Certainly since the second half of the last century, everything's become left hemisphere-led. But I think the world is beginning to appreciate brains like ours. When I'm doing timeline work with clients, I might have them go right back to the moment they arrived on planet Earth, metaphorically of course. Because you know, what is the potential any of us are born with when we arrive here? What is that stardust that's within us? And if that potential illuminated all the way through our time on the planet, what would be possible for us?

And then I scoop them along to the other end of their timeline and say, "Okay, so you've lived your most optimised, wonderful, everything possible life, what did that look like?" Those are great questions because they set the brain up to possibility. There have to be a few mechanical steps in there, because if somebody just sits in dreamland without propulsion or tenacity, the skills to move forward, they don't get very far. And of course a lot of artists

Chapter two: Alexander Millar

get stuck and trapped in that state of inertia because they're overwhelmed by all those beautiful possibilities, and they can't get themselves moving forward.

Alexander: That's right. Going back to my dad, he was very Victorian in his outlook. You know, children should be seen and not heard. And he had a lot of baggage. He was illegitimate, and in the 1930s and 1940s, there was a very different attitude towards kids like him. And when you're carrying baggage, you'll look for somebody to dump it on, you know? So I became the dumping ground.

I always remember my school reports. I wasn't very academic, but if had an A-grade on my report and showed it to him, he would say, "It should have been an A*." It was so demoralising. I used to joke with him that my gravestone would say: "Here lies Alexander Millar. Could have lived longer."

And it's that thing that my dad instilled in me, because I didn't get on with him, especially in my teens. I couldn't stand him to be honest, but I kind of got to know the man and I was friends with him before he died. But it always remained with us – I could have done better. So every painting I did, I could hear my dad, "You could have done better." So every painting was like, "I'm going to show you. I'm going to show you that I'm good." I still use it today. It drives me to excel.

As you say, never put limits on where your timeline might end. It should go on – to be the best, to be the greatest. Listen to Muhammad Ali: "I am the greatest." He talked the talk and walked the walk. He was the greatest, and he made sure he told everybody. Whatever skill or talent you have, self-belief will take you such a distance in your life. And in those travels, the doors will present themselves to you.

Chapter two: Alexander Millar

Kay: You're the best at being you, and every one of us is doing the best we can right now with what we've got. So, what if we continue to be the best of us? And then what… and then what… and then what? For me, that's what self-belief is.

You mention your dad a lot, and I know how important both your parents were to you, or are to you, and there's something about those early paintings that connected you to your early years in Springside, near Glasgow. Over the years, through the conversations I've had with you, I know a lot of your paintings are you going into your inner world. I wonder if a lot of artists do this. Maybe you're expressing something and redefining it, connecting the dots or making sense of it?

Alexander: I'm kind of making sense of it for myself initially. And that's important, because if you don't feel it yourself, you'll never be able to express on the canvas. Somebody asked me recently, "Do you realise your painting is done from the perspective of a child's eyes?" And I said yes, because the paintings are actually looking up to the characters. And again, it's an unconscious thing, I hadn't realised at the time, but my happiest times were in Springside. It's a little mining community just outside Kilmarnock and it's never changed. If you've ever watched *The Quiet Man* with John Wayne and Maureen O'Hara, that's my childhood. Those are the kind of people I was born and brought up with. And because I was a kid and had no responsibilities, it was a secure, safe time. I think that's what I try to express in my paintings. From a child's point of view, I want to wrap myself up in that warm blanket of safety and security and nostalgia.

The only way I can express it to the students who ask for advice is to say you can learn the mechanics of painting, the composition, mixing colours, but you have to paint from the heart. Everything

Chapter two: Alexander Millar

is energy and vibration. And whatever is vibrating here in your heart, you will put in, and it will stay in the canvas. And it resonates with people, and that's why people stood and cried at my work.

I did a painting of the shipyard. It was a ship being launched and all the old men were on there in their flat caps. It was on show in Glasgow, and this guy was in floods of tears. Billy, the guy who works with me, had to sit the old fella down. He said he worked in the shipyards and the narrative in his life was that when they launched a ship, it was a moment of pride, but they weren't sure if that was going to be the last ship they'd ever work on. So he saw himself and all his friends who were no longer alive in that painting. So there was a resonance that hit him, that made the emotional connection.

"You can learn the mechanics of painting, the composition, mixing colours, but you have to paint from the heart. Everything is energy and vibration"

So that's what I have to say to anybody who wants to take up art. Paint from the heart. You have to paint something that moves you, because the resonance you've got in yourself will resonate on the canvas. And that's the little key that unlocks the difference between something that's – okay, I hate to use the word – ordinary, and something extraordinary.

Even though my work is quite naïve, there's something extraordinary, and that's something I've come across accidentally.

Chapter two: Alexander Millar

When I understood it, I thought, "Oh, there's the key to it." It's almost like miners when they come across a vein of gold. They're chipping and chipping and mining it and then they come to the tiny little vein of gold and go, "Oh, there it is!"

Everything in life's a bit like that, especially the creative side, whether it's music or art or whatever. It's that little vein. You don't know how long it's going to last. It could go on forever. It might not. You just have to use it while you can.

Kay: I think something very important in what you're saying is that when you operate in your heart space, in that vibration or emotional space, then you have to have dropped down out of your head space. So in order to drop down out of the thinking mind, the internal dialogue – "Oh that's not very good, blah, blah" – and you come down to that expression that comes out through the limbic system of our brain and the heart space, the emotional space, when you're operating from there, the flow is there, isn't it? The freedom is there. My question is, do you do something to prepare yourself, to bring yourself down out of your thinking mind?

Alexander: Yes, when I draw. I try to sketch every day. Before lockdown, I used to go to a café in Newcastle called Arlo's. It's very busy, with lots of people and lots of buzz. And oddly enough, that takes me from a thinking state to a trance-like one. It's like when you talk to someone on the phone and you're doodling, but you don't realise what you're doing. That's the state you have to be in when you're drawing.

At the café, there's all this buzz and activity, people say hello, and I find that beneficial for me to work in, oddly, because it takes me out of concentrating too much on what I'm doing to, "Oh, what's going on over there…" coming back and then, "Oh, aye."

Chapter two: Alexander Millar

You know, you can sit in a café and try and sketch and somebody is going to be looking at you and then you think, "Somebody's looking, oh no…" But it's a reversal for me. Maybe I'm a born performer. I find it easier to take myself out of myself and let it flow. That's where the flow is. And that helps me to go back into the studio to paint. When you're painting, the magic happens when you're not thinking, when you're in the trance, the flow state. That's my way of working – go for a coffee, start sketching, and sketching takes me into the painting. I sketch, sketch, sketch, sketch, draw. That's the way to do it.

Kay: And switch your mind off?

Alexander: Switch it off, yeah. Stop thinking. Just do.

Kay: I have clients who get creative blocks and I ask, "Oh, I wonder how you do that?" and then unpick their strategy, and the blocks are created by their thoughts.

Alexander: If I have an artistic block, I need to stop painting, go for a walk and do something entirely different, then come back. And I always paint to music. It's nothing structured. I like music that's hypnotic, that allows you to let go. Your conscious can listen to the music and then let you get on with it.

Kay: You know, I spend a lot of my life helping people to change their brainwaves and brain chemistry so they get that clarity and access to their whole brain and whole self.

A while ago, we were talking about being able to express something through artwork, and I was reminded of some research I read a few years after 9/11. It showed that children who had

Chapter two: Alexander Millar

successfully readjusted after the trauma of having witnessed the Twin Towers attack were the children who, during play therapy and art therapy, had come up with solutions in their minds. So they were able to draw trampolines or parachutes to catch the people falling out of the buildings. It's like their unconscious mind took over and helped them to make sense of what their sensory experience had been. As a result of that, the brain could go, "Okay, that's taken care of, I don't need to think about it anymore. Move on."

And that's very simplistic because, you know, there's more to trauma de-coding than that, but I like to remind people that our story-telling minds are always trying to make sense of what we are experiencing. That was on my mind when you were talking earlier about that need to make sense of your childhood, your relationship with your father and so on. But it also brings me to the subject of 9/11. And on the back of that, you had a very successful exhibition in New York City.

Alexander: Yes, that was fascinating. It started when I watched an interview with a lady named Pearl Maynard. She spoke of that morning of 9/11, listening to her son get ready for work. He was in his early 20s, he was called Keithroy Maynard. He used to sing his favourite song every morning to get ready, and

> *"She said, 'You know what it is… here's a guy in a kilt 6,000 miles away and he's the only one that sees me and what I do'. And that touched me"*

Chapter two: Alexander Millar

he was instrumental in getting a lot of young black kids into the fire service. So he was singing his favourite song, *America*, and he was getting ready. He had a little boy himself, but still lived with his mum. And he said bye to his mum and that was the last day she saw him because he was killed in the North Tower when it collapsed.

My heart went out to her, so I did a painting. Instead of an old gadgie, I made him a firefighter. A New York firefighter. And you know the uniforms they wear, the protective garb, have black and yellow stripes around and their name on? Well, I put Maynard on it and on the helmet his ladder (the yards where they work are called ladders). So I put Ladder 33, that was his ladder number. And he had the American flag draped on him and he was carrying a wee boy.

I forget how it happened now, but we got in touch with the New York Fire Department, and we were looking for a way to do an exhibition in New York for their charity. And it was like the universe went, "Okay, this is going to happen." So I did an exhibition based on the firefighters.

I met a lady called Regina Wilson. She's the head of a fraternity inside the New York Fire Department called the Vulcan Society. It's like a union for the black firefighters, and I decided to make all my firefighters black. Now Regina is the first female black president, and she was in tears because I showed her some of the paintings. And she says, "You know what it is… here's a guy in a kilt 6,000 miles away, and he's the only one that sees me and what I do."

And that touched me. That touched me a lot. So I decided to do more. And I did a big painting of what was remaining of the Twin Towers and I took the image of the American soldiers raising the flag at Iwo Jima, but the figures are made into firefighters

Chapter two: Alexander Millar

with the backdrop of the Twin Towers. It's quite emotive. Out of 343 firefighters who died, there were 12 black firefighters, and they don't get recognised. They don't get a mention. And when I was talking to the firefighters out there, the black firefighters were saying that when the press came around to take photographs, you know, pulling dead bodies out of the rubble and all sorts, as soon as they saw they were black, they would stop taking photographs of them and find white firefighters. That's awful. Shocking.

So the names that I put in the four figures raising the flag, I took them from the black firefighters who died. And Keithroy Maynard's name was in there. And when we came to have the show at the New York Fire Department Museum, there were lots of people there for the opening night, talking and blathering away, and suddenly the crowd parted and there was this old black lady standing and crying at this painting of Keithroy Maynard. And it was Pearl. It was like seeing my mum again, and I just went up and put my arm around her. And all the work I had put into that exhibition, it made it all worthwhile, just to see her. And I said to her, "This is Keithroy's painting."

We never really know how we touch other people's lives, but when your work touches lives in ways you may never know, it spurs you on. Every person who says, "That's my grandfather, that's my dad, my mum..." whatever. And when they stand and cry at the paintings, that assures me that whatever I'm doing in the work is right.

Kay: But you know, there's something else in what you're saying. I know you have a great sense of humour and having watched you rise to some dizzy heights and hang out with all sorts of celebrities, none of it has gone to your head. You're still very humble, fun and straightforward. How do you do that?

Chapter two: Alexander Millar

Alexander: I always remember Denise Robertson, who was the agony aunt on the *This Morning* show on ITV in the UK. A lovely old lady, she's gone now, and she bought a few paintings from me over the years. When you're meeting all those famous people, I can see how it could go to somebody's head and change them as people. And Denise said, "Make sure you keep both feet on the ground." And I joked with her. I said, "If I can keep one foot on the ground, then the other one can roam free."

I think of my formative years. There was an old man called Phil Todd and he was a great Robbie Burns aficionado who could recite every poem. Anyway, they used to call me Sandy back then. I remember one time, because I always love going back to the village because my auntie still lives there and I love wandering around the place because every corner holds a memory, and Phil Todd says, "Sandy, they can take the boy out of Springside, but they'll never take Springside out of the boy." And it's very true. It's a leveller. And that's a good place to be.

It's like any moment in your journey. You can have ups and downs and twists and bends, but there are points where nothing else matters and you've taken in this wonderful view which costs you nothing; it's just arrived in front of you. And having been brought up in that small village makes you realise that you can have this, that and the other, but don't forget the important things in your life. And the important things are your happiness, your family, whether you're loved. It's those little things; the little things are the big things.

And I guess my upbringing, even though my dad was hard on me, has been a good learning curve. And being Scottish, humour plays a big part. We're very self-deprecating. Look at our football team! There's a great video. Scotland were playing Poland and were beaten 2-0 and the Tartan Army was coming out the

Chapter two: Alexander Millar

stadium and they were having a great time. They were playing the bagpipes, hugging the opposing fans, shaking hands and kissing them. We'd been beaten 2-0, and the opposing fans were astounded that we were having a party because win, lose or draw, we've made a whole lot of new friends, we've had a great time, we've watched a game of football.

And that's what's instilled in you in Scotland. If you win, great. If you draw, great. If you lose, great. You've had a good time; don't think too much of yourself. And if you do, there's always something that will bring you down. There's a lot to be said for your nationality, your background. And don't forget it.

Kay: From my view, you understand yourself well and make the best of what you have and where you're at. You've taken the time to figure out your bit of life. I've noticed that whomever you've rubbed shoulders with, you're aware of them and what's true for them, but you've always been comfortable with who you are.

Alexander: I got to know everybody, I mean all the big stars and stuff in LA, and a lot of them are very fragile, worried about their star being in the descendancy. And that's something outside them. They become so worried about that, and they tend to forget who they are. I was invited once to Brit Week. It's a celebration of all the Britishness in Los Angeles and Tony Blair was hosting it. They wanted me to auction one of my paintings to raise money for charity. Everybody was talking about Blair and like, "Wow, he used to be Prime Minister of England," and I had my kilt on and I came out and I said to him, "Ho, bonnie lad, Newcastle are having a shit season this year," and he burst out laughing, but that was just coming back to who you are.

I had a long chat with Kiefer Sutherland about his music. That

Chapter two: Alexander Millar

was him, he was the star of *24*, but he was more interested in his music. It's when you get rid of all the stardom and just, you know, have a nice chat. I'm going to name drop here, but I had a nice chat with Robert Plant because he lived up the road and we went out for dinner. And it was odd because you know, he's done everything in his career, and I said to him, "Robert, what do you really want to do, now you've done everything?" And he said, "I really want to have a go at building a dry-stone wall." And I was like, of all the things he wants to do, he wants to learn how to be a dry stone waller? Who would have thought?

> *"That's what's instilled in you in Scotland. If you win, great. If you draw, great. if you lose, great. You've had a good time; don't think too much of yourself"*

Kay: This brings us back to the point where you talk about painting from your heart, your feelings, your emotions. And it sounds like so long as you stay connected to that place, then you can remain authentic in the world. And I think when people disconnect from that place, instead of trusting their feelings they trust what the outside world is saying about them. That can cause a lot of trouble, can't it?

Alexander: Yeah, the whole structure of Los Angeles is so based on the film industry. That's why Daniel Day Lewis will come and shoot in Los Angeles but go straight back to Ireland, because that's

Chapter two: Alexander Millar

where he's grounded. Hollywood is a strange place. It was nice going and seeing everything and meeting everybody there, but coming back was nicer. There's nae place like home.

Kay: Exactly. And yes, you meet the same people on the way up as you do on the way down. But if you meet people who you resonate with, whether you adhere to or buy into any sort of hierarchical structure of movement up or down or whatever, when you just connect then it's easy, isn't it? And it's authentic.

Alexander: Well, I take life with a pinch of salt. Because as you say, it's just part of the road you're on with your ups and downs and twists and turns. And whenever something exciting happens in your life, just take a moment to enjoy it. Just add that pinch of salt, because it will preserve it and flavour it and enhance everything about it. And at the same time it'll keep you grounded.

www.alexandermillar.com

Chapter two: Alexander Millar

Chapter three: Kathleen La Valle

KATHLEEN LA VALLE

Kathleen La Valle is a Licensed Master Trainer of NLP™ and DHE® and has been conducting training and development seminars for more than 30 years. She runs the international training team that supports Dr Richard Bandler and John La Valle where she inspires us with her love of training, care and concern for her students while teaching us all to venture beyond limitations. We chatted twice mid 2020 and this is an amalgam of those two interviews where we discuss the role of metaphor and creativity in helping others flourish.

Chapter three: Kathleen La Valle

Kay: We've been chatting about creativity recently, and I'm wondering if you feel that creativity is in your blood, or is it something that evolved for you?

Kathleen: Well I think when we look at the word creativity, we're looking at a nominalisation [a thing], as we say in NLP and in linguistics. For me, creativity isn't a thing. I think there's a problem when people say, "Oh, I'm not creative, I don't have creativity; that person has creativity, I don't know how to be creative." And I think that's because it has become a thing.

It reminds me of business situations, when people say, "Oh, we need communication…" and they have meetings and discuss the meaning of communication and it becomes a thing, and they forget how to turn it into a process. And when you realise it's a process, it's something that you can do. It's therefore something you can learn to do.

That's easier than trying to acquire creativity, because as you turn it into a thing, the brain goes, "Creativity! Do I have it? Do I don't have it? I don't know how to get it." So you begin to even question whether or not you're creative when you say the word creativity, because by turning it into a thing, your brain has to say, "Do I possess this? Do I own this? How much of it do I own?" And that's not what you should be focused on as someone wanting to build creativity; you want to build the process of doing it.

So what does it take to be a creator? What do you do to create? How do you create? And just learning about creating – creating things, creating ideas, creating paintings, creating writing that has a flow to it – all as opposed to, "Oh, let's talk about creativity."

So I think creativity is a great overall topic, and the next step has to be, let's talk about the process of doing it. So, how do we begin to create? And if you don't think you have this process

Chapter three: Kathleen La Valle

nailed down, then find fun ways to practise it. I'll give you a quick example: Kay, you're part of a wonderful team of trainers who support Dr Bandler's trainings and our [John and Kathleen La Valle] trainings. And one of the things we do as a team is we play a fun game that most people probably would think is a joke. But you know I always have an ulterior motive, and one of the funny games we play that's actually a practice for creativity is somebody says, "Oh, I'm tired of being cooped up in my room." And then somebody goes, "Well you know, at least you came here in order to wing it." And then somebody else goes, "Well birds of a feather, you know?"

And the next thing you know, we're running all these puns that are building around 'coop', chicken coop. Like, "At least you didn't chicken out." So this goes around the room, and we all laugh, which is great brain chemistry, and we have good fun with it. And actually, that in itself is a great exercise to do for building creation, building the process of being able to create something.

Everybody's laughing, having a good time, and we're sharing all these puns and putting out all these different ambiguities, connecting to different places in our brain at the same time. And that's the beauty about ambiguities; they're the structure of humour. I'm not talking about jokes, I'm talking about the structure of humour. When you say a word like 'check', for example, it can go to different places in the brain.

Take this business example: 30 years ago John and I had a chiropractor who let us use his consultation room to see clients. In trade, we would help him out with some of his issues in the office or we'd do talks for his patients. So one day he comes to us and he says, "I have a perfect new receptionist. I love her, my office loves her, which is really unusual because nobody likes the new girl you bring in. Everybody adores her. The patients adore her. I adore

Chapter three: Kathleen La Valle

her. She's doing a great job. But she won't ask patients for money."

So we talked to her, and she really was uncomfortable asking for money. So patients were coming in, booking their next appointment, leaving and never paying. These days at doctors' offices, you pay up front, before the session. But back then, they let you pay after the session. So they would come say goodbye, book the next appointment and walk out the door. So we said to her, "Hey, let's play a funny game the next time somebody comes in." She had this big book in front of her, and we said, "The next time somebody comes along, put your hand out like this (palm up) and say, 'let me check on your next appointment'."

And people would unconsciously go, "Oh, that's right, I have to pay you." Or they'd just start going into their wallet while they were agreeing the next date. Well, she thought that was so funny that she eventually started coming up with her own games. That's because we looked at it as a game, something she could be creative with, something she could develop. So she started calling me and telling me the different ways she was doing it.

Basically, in that example, the 'check' on your next appointment was also 'check', meaning to write a (US) check to pay. So you had that same word that goes to two parts of the brain. Kay, you laughed when I said it because the brain finds it funny when you run an ambiguity where a word goes to two places at the same time. For some reason, it's like going inside and tickling your brain.

So if you do that creativity exercise where somebody starts a topic, say, "So I was getting ready to wash my hair," and somebody goes, "Well, I hope you didn't wig out," and somebody says, "Well, you know, when you comb through what you had to do today…" And you start going around the room like that. You can do it on Zoom or Teams, you can do it if you have kids in the family. And you can keep track because maybe the first time you only come up

Chapter three: Kathleen La Valle

with five or six before you run out, then maybe you get to the point where you can do 10 or 15 or 20 before you run out of words. So it's a great way to measure how well you're working in building this creativity.

Kay: I love that game. In our family, it'll spark off out of nowhere, and the more we do it, the more spontaneity and laughter flows.

Kathleen: The whole point is fun. This isn't something where you're going to take out the books of creativity and look up on the internet the definition of creativity and do all this long research about exactly what is required in this to be fun. The more you make creativity fun, the more your brain is going to want to do it.

Also, creativity knows no media. So if you want to be more creative in your thinking, it doesn't mean you can't paint to be more creative. It doesn't mean you can't sculpt to be more creative. It doesn't mean you can't build something with wood and hammers and nails to be more creative. It knows no media; it's just about exercising the brain so that when you're looking at something and then you're seeing how it comes out, you're feeling how it's coming out, you're hearing how it comes out. It's about having this multi-sensory experience of doing something, of creating something.

Kay: I think creativity is our most natural state.

Kathleen: Absolutely. I run a session in our NLP Master Practitioner training prep session, where I remind people that as a child, we had so much experience of experiencing the world. We wanted to taste it, we wanted to see it, we wanted to smell it, we wanted to feel it – everything was a wonder. As adults we slowly

Chapter three: Kathleen La Valle

lose that wonder and things become habitual, and I think that goes against that grain of creating.

When you want to go against the grain of creating, then you go into habit. So anything that's a habit, if you change it, you're creating something new. So if you look at the way you do something, even brushing your teeth, and look at what can you do to change that, so you're creating something different and still brushing your teeth as well, what can you do? It's just a simple thing.

I was talking to my son about hand-washing. With children, they say wash your hands for two *Happy Birthday* songs. So what if every day you picked something else to be having a birthday? Today is my toothbrush's birthday, so happy birthday dear toothbrush, happy birthday to you… And the next day it's the faucet. Happy birthday dear faucet, happy birthday to you… And every day you pick something new rather than just remotely reciting the happy birthday song.

Every day you're singing *Happy Birthday* and every time you wash your hands, it's boring. But if you pick something funny and different each day, say it's the shower curtain's birthday today – happy birthday, dear shower curtain. You can do anything to make things more fun and then you're creating something out of an old habit.

Kay: And there's something about the chemistry of laughter, which this brings me on to NHR®. One of the Bandler® Technologies is NHR® [Neuro Hypnotic Repatterning®] and it's my absolute favourite because it's the creation of wonderful brain chemistry and energies in whichever direction we choose. Tell me a little bit about how you perceive that, as I know that you do it so beautifully on stage.

Chapter three: Kathleen La Valle

Kathleen: Well, one of the things I like to do with trainers who are at a seminar supporting us is a little trance before we start the day. That's about resources; the resources you need for the day. And this might be a fun thing to do in the morning when you first wake up, to know the resources you think you might need today. So the first thing might be we're going to need to stay patient or be able to organise things because, you know, you have a busy schedule. So we think, "Oh, I've got to organise my schedule and prioritise," or whatever words you want to use. And then when you think about that, how does that feel? How does that process feel? And what's that resource feeling when you're feeling very organised or you're feeling you can put things in sequence and in order – how does that make you feel?

We can use any kind of metaphor you want. I usually use a cauldron. I think about a big pot or cauldron and it's bubbling. And I talk about, "Okay so let's take that solution down…" Oh, and 'solution' – there's another one of those phonological ambiguities or puns. It's a solution, meaning a liquid, something suspended in liquid, and it's also a solution to your day. You need organisation or you need to prioritise schedules or organise things. And you put some of that in that cauldron.

> *"What we say is that you're your own bartender. You're mixing your own brain cocktail, so what do you need in your brain that day? What's the solution?"*

Chapter three: Kathleen La Valle

And I have people do that in detail; so they see what the bottle is, or the dropper, or is it a shaker? Is it a powder, is it a pouch you take out to fit in whatever you want to do, and then think is that enough? What else would I want in this day? So maybe I'm going to need a good sense of humour because I've got a lot of things to get done in a short amount of time. So I'm probably going to need my best sense of humour available. So you reach up and you pull out that sense of humour solution and you dump that in, and then you go, oh maybe a little more of that. And you go through this process of thinking, what else do I need? Okay, patience; I need to be able to stop and breathe some patience powder in there. You can make it as fun as you want; you're building the solution.

Basically, what you're doing is you're creating, and in the end what we say is that you're your own bartender. You're mixing your own brain cocktail. So what cocktail do you need in your brain that day? What's the solution? So what other things might you need?

You have some patience, so add some sense of humour. You have some prioritising, organising skills. What else do you need to have? Maybe some ability to tune up your senses so that you're seeing opportunities and the best ways to move things.

And we're hearing the tone in the voice; sensory ability, sensory acuity. "Okay, so let's take that down and put that in there and begin stirring it all and mixing it so that you're taking things that you normally wouldn't be putting together and making this great solution."

In training we might do this in trance with someone. Then I tell them to take out their ladle and dip it in and take a big sip and feel that solution running through your body and your brain so that you're ready to organise the day. You're going to be having great sensory acuity. You see all those opportunities to make things fit, make things work easily. You have lots of sense of humour, you

Chapter three: Kathleen La Valle

know when to stop and then move into the next piece. So you're building that solution.

So many times in NHR®, people say to me, "Well, I'm still working with this…" And we say, "What do you sense then?" So somebody might say to you, "I want to be motivated." And then somebody goes, "Oh, yeah, I'm going to be motivated." In NLP, we say, "Okay, great, every time you feel motivated, you can feel the motivating feeling. So what do you see? What do you hear? What do you feel when you're in that motivating place?" And you know, you do all the stuff; you can anchor it or build it into a strategy, which is all good stuff and healthy.

But in NHR® we say, "That's it, you want to be motivated, really? That's it? So what else can we do with that? Well, let's look at motivated for a moment. So you're motivated, you're highly motivated, you're moving forward, you're out there, you're in your group, and all of a sudden you hit an obstacle. Now what? All you know is to go forward."

So we'd also say, "What if you were creatively motivated to do the meeting? What if you were motivated creatively so that when you ran forward and you hit that obstacle, creativity kicks in to go, 'What do I do with this? I can make this from it. I can move it around. I can go under it. I can go over it. I can go through it. I can utilise it to do something else'."

So when you mix creativity with motivation, now you have something that has less chance of getting railroaded, of getting blocked, because you mixed creativity into motivating, and creating and motivating work hand in hand together.

So that's some of the things that in NHR® we look at, and which fits perfectly. We're talking in terms of being able to be in a place where you can create. When you're motivating yourself to move and you get stuck, you don't want to have to then stop and de-rail yourself and figure out what to do; you want that creative process right alongside so that it just jumps in and takes over. So blending motivating and creating is a great resource.

Kay: I love that, and I'm such a fan of NHR®. When I was introduced to it, I was like 'Aha'; the concept that you can design how you want to feel before you get there. Wow! Why didn't I know that?

Kathleen: Yes, I was like, "Duh, why didn't I do this when I was in school and high school, even college; this would have been great information to have." And all the technologies that Richard's developing have blown me away.

Kay: It's just an endless, wonderful exploration of our minds, bodies and spirits.

Kathleen: It absolutely is. And since we're talking about creating, you can even create new feelings you've never felt before. The first time I was in an NHR® seminar, Richard was on stage and

"We're talking in terms of being able to be in a place where you can create. When you're motivating yourself to move and you get stuck, you don't want to have to then stop and de-rail yourself and figure out what to do"

Chapter three: Kathleen La Valle

he said, "And this afternoon, we're going to create new feelings." And I was like, what? And I'd already been in NLP for like 20 years. I was like, "How are we going do to that? Do we have to go to Mars or something to create new feelings?" And it was simply some of the things that we had already learned. Design Human Engineering®, another of Dr Bandler's technologies, was just basically breaking down some of those modalities and mixing them.

You know, if you take your heart rate from passion and mix it with the way you see things in motivating states and in the way you hear things in curiosity and learning and mix those together, you've got a new state just by mixing the different submodalities. And that blew me away because the possibilities are infinite.

Kay: If only we'd had those skills as children, can you imagine what the world would be like? I don't know exactly how it is in the States or globally, but certainly in the UK we have an education system that just steals a lot of fun or creativity. So we churn out these teenagers who take life terribly seriously.
A lot of my focus and attention right now is on trying to ease these skills into the minds of young people.

Kathleen: It's very frustrating for us. When John and I first started this, we wanted to do some community give-back locally here in New Jersey. We went around the school system, and we said, "We'll come in any afternoon, 3pm, 4pm, whatever you want, and we'll do an hour, two hours, three hours, whatever you guys want as teachers, and we can show you how to teach kids how to spell in like five minutes. We can show you how to help students that are struggling." And you know how many schools took us up on it? Not many.

Chapter three: Kathleen La Valle

Later, when we started the NLP Practitioner programmes, teachers or people working within the school system would come, and afterwards they'd come back and say, "Could you please come in and work with our teachers or teach our teachers? And we actually need an NLP Practitioner programme for only teachers." And that was the worst training; it was that thing – doctors make the worst patients, and teachers make the worst students.

And bless the teachers, all of you out there, I know you have such an important role and we love you, but oh my God, we had a room full of teachers and every day it was the same thing: "Did you guys practise the language patterns we asked you to do last night?" And we'd get, "Well, you know, I got home and my dog had to go for a walk…" Or they were chatting during the class, getting up and moving around the room. I'm like, "Guys, just get in your groups, get started on the exercise," you know? And they were like, "But we don't want to do the exercises."

I said, "Are you hearing this? Any of this sound familiar to any of you?" Because when you hear them, they're chit-chatting in their breaks and constantly complaining about their classes, how Billy won't sit there and his homework is always late.

But they loved the work. They loved the training. And they were all angry at their colleges. They were like, "Why don't they teach us this in teaching college? If they had showed me this when I was teaching college, it would have made a big difference." And they were angry that nobody showed them this. It goes back to things versus process. We talk about the things, and the processes never go deep enough, we don't dive into exploring them. When I look at a process, I look at it like putting on something; putting on a costume or whatever. I put on the process, I live in it, and I look through its eyes. I possess it, so when I see a process, I want to get in it.

When people are talking and I'm listening to how they're doing

Chapter three: Kathleen La Valle

something a certain way or how they're framing something a certain way, then I immediately start trying it on because I'm just trying to figure out how they could come up with it.

So I've got to go in and try it on because I don't see how it's possible for somebody to get to that conclusion or to that point. I dip in and come back out, and I'm constantly floating into it and trying it on and looking through their eyes and their filters, then coming back out and going, "Okay, well, there's one piece of that I like; the rest they can keep." And sometimes that gets me into trouble, but basically I'm constantly trying to try things on, different processes, because I think that's that creative flow that you want to be able to experience things in new ways.

So anything that you do differently, as I said before; we find a different way to take a habit and turn it into something more fun, then it's great. And we know on a simple basis this works. You don't like mopping the floor, but if you put a song on and you mop the floor and dance while you're mopping, the mopping is more fun. I mean, these are basic, simple things we can do to take a habit and be creative about it, making it more fun, making you feel better so you want to do it, you enjoy the process of doing it.

And we can take that same system into bigger models. The first

"These are basic, simple things we can do to take a habit and be creative about it, making it more fun, making you feel better so you want to do it, you enjoy the process of doing it"

Chapter three: Kathleen La Valle

thing with anything that's habitual, is that you want to be able to find a different way to do it; that's going to crack that opening in the wall that you can begin to see a new way, come up with a new process. Or come up with a new creativity model to come up with a new way of enjoying the process, if it's something that you don't enjoy, or something you want to be more motivated about doing. And I keep coming back to that – getting rid of those habitual things in our lives.

Kay: But you have to want to do that, don't you?

Kathleen: And if you're a coach your job is to find an entry point. First of all, you need a basic rapport. And I don't mean you have to sit there and match the way they're sitting, breathing and all that stuff; but you have to earn that right to influence them in some way, and dangle a big enough carrot that there's a reason to do it differently.

I always listen to what they're saying. They'll say, "Oh well, you know, my husband never listens to me. No one takes me seriously…" So they tell me all the things that are messed up and I say, "So what are you doing to fix that?" And they go, "Well, I do this at work and now I do this and that hasn't really happened." And I'm like, "Okay, so all the ways you've tried so far haven't helped. So what if I could show you something that's probably going to sound crazy, probably going to sound really different, but you know what, if I gave you a crazy idea to do, would you be willing to do it?"

So I'm going to put that up against the fact that they just told me all the things that don't work, and then of course we want to find out what they do want instead. None of that stuff that they're doing is moving them towards what they want, "So what if I told

Chapter three: Kathleen La Valle

you something crazy to do? Would you be willing to try it?" That's my strategy with getting them to try something new.

And the meditation part – we've all been talking about it on the news and in the interviews we've done so far during this situation. We just keep talking about the fact that you need to meditate, you need to relax. We need to expand your mind so that you can keep your body healthy. And these are all parts of the process. If you get people out of their body, you get people out of their normal mindset to do something different. If you don't meditate, do something like a visualisation process. Those are things that you can practise to get yourself out of the rut of what you're doing.

Kay: Relaxation, visualisation and meditation can be such easy ways to help people open up to their inner wisdom.

Kathleen: It's simple. A lot of times I talk to people and I only have maybe a few minutes with them on a phone call or an email or something. And they're overwhelmed and they're really stressing out. And I literally tell them to do the sound "Ahhhhh" because these are things that are hard-wired within us. If you just stop for a moment and just go, "Ahhhh…" Making that sound automatically cools things down; you can feel it in your forehead and your scalp, you can feel it sometimes down your arms. If you've done it well enough, your muscles relax because it's hard-wired. As Richard says, when you're done with a meal, you push back from the table and you go, "Ahhhhh…" You know, it's that sense of everything's okay, everything is completed, we're done, it's over. And that's such a powerful hardwire.

So if you actually do it on purpose, you still get the brain, the body connection to that sound. And you can do it even better. You can learn to vibrate that off deeper down into your chest, your

Chapter three: Kathleen La Valle

diaphragm, to use your throat fully. When you're making that sound, the better you become at it. You can immediately trigger that cool-down process.

Sometimes if I see a lot of stress or tension, I'll tell someone they have to breathe the breath of the dragon. So one of the exhales has to be like you're breathing fire from the dragon. But when you're doing that, you're taking all the stress from your body and you're building it up. And when you exhale, you breathe it out in flames. So the flames just burn all the stress. So you have to do that really loud. I tell them to do that, to go take a deep breath this time and instead of sighing, I want you to breathe out like a dragon with fire and take all that stress and watch it burn in the flames. When you breathe out, the people laugh and they think it's funny, but they've never allowed themselves to breathe like a dragon, because as an adult you don't do those things anymore.

Kay: I love that... The breath of a dragon, what fun!

Kathleen: We have to remind ourselves as adults that we can still do things creatively and fun. We had a newscaster here in the States who was working from home during this pandemic and that didn't work out so well. He moved, pulled back just for a moment, and the viewers could see his boxer shorts underneath his dress shirt and tie. There was a weatherman on the news yesterday, and up front he said, "Look, my wife has a Zoom meeting in the other room, so I have the girls with me and they promised they're going to sit here on the couch and they're going to be good." He said, "They want to say hi, so I'm going to let them come out and say hi." So these two little heads appear, and he introduces them and he says, "Okay, girls, now go sit down."

And he starts the weather and they have that green screen

Chapter three: Kathleen La Valle

behind him with the weather map thing. And that lasted three seconds before you see these hands starting to appear, and this little one is about three and she's climbing up his suit. So now he's got the one on this arm and the other one's head keeps popping in the shot, and now she's walking where the weather is that he's reporting, so he's trying to get her to move. I was in tears, I thought it was great. And he came back and apologised later. And I was like, dude, there was nothing to apologise for. I got the weather. I got everything you said you wanted me to hear. And I laughed. I don't usually laugh through weather reports. I thought it was fabulous. I think they should do the weather that way all the time. Bring in kids, dogs, elephants, giraffes. I don't care!

Kay: You remind us that there's so much fun to be found, even in serious times. You said before you try on a process you feel it, that playfulness is such an important attribute. Again, do you think that's just something that is your go-to, or have you learned to unlearn not being playful in order to be playful?

Kathleen: I think I'm playful for a lot of different reasons. One is that I was an only child, so I had to make up for the fact that I didn't have sisters and

> *"I have the Peter Pan gene – I have to grow old, but I don't have to grow up. I take my work seriously, my clients' customer service seriously, but I don't have to take it in a serious way"*

Chapter three: Kathleen La Valle

brothers to play with, so I found all kinds of ways to have company or to play. Whether it was imaginary characters, my dolls, my toys.

My favourite toy when I was really young was a cardboard box. Maybe it's the Leo in me – being a cat. I loved back then that they would bring home the groceries in cardboard boxes from the store. I would sit there patiently waiting for them to empty that box, and I would draw things on the side of the box like little portholes and it would be a boat ride, or wings and it would be a plane. And I'd sit in the box and go on journeys with it.

I have the Peter Pan gene – I have to grow old, but I don't have to grow up. I take my work seriously, my clients' customer service seriously, but I don't have to take it in a serious way. And that's where being creative helps, because I find creative ways of making it fun, whatever I have to do. I make a crazy imagination thing in my brain out of it. So that's where the whole creating space helps. In terms of when you're doing serious things, you get creative about it. It makes them less serious.

Kay: In NLP we explore strategies, and I wonder what you would say is your favourite strategy for doing creativity?

Kathleen: I'm constantly asking myself, "Can I make this fun?" That's my mantra, "Can I make this fun?" If it's not going to be fun, then I have to go back and tweak my strategy until I can find a way to make it fun, because then I know I have a better chance of success.

A message I have for people out there who are stressing out is that this is a great opportunity to create, I wouldn't say a new you because you've got a great you, and it can always use some polishing, some dressing up, some added abilities. And this is the time to do it. So always make it fun; this is the time to do things

Chapter three: Kathleen La Valle

you'd never think you'd have done before. If you don't dance, this is a great time to learn how to dance. You can do it alone in your room. You can just turn music on and move your body until it feels full-on. This is the time to get some art supplies and put some great music on and just move the brush to the music with different colours and see what comes out. This isn't the time to take anything seriously. This is the time to play. This is the time to be playful.

Think about the animals, the baby animals, the puppies and the kittens and foxes and everything. They all play fight. They all learn by playing. And now you have an opportunity to stay home and try new things. So paint, draw, write, do poetry, sing songs, write songs; things that you wouldn't normally do. Get some clay and mould things. You can do anything. Cook or bake – there are so many recipes and videos about how to make this, how to make that. So this is the time to try new things because every time you try something new, you grow a new cortical pathway. So every time you play, every time you try something new, every moment is an opportunity to grow a new cortical pathway and you never know where that new cortical pathway can take you.

Kay: I love the metaphor of baby animals play-fighting. It reminds me of the fun we have in our team, simply playing with metaphor.

Kathleen: One time, I challenged you all to take the fewest words possible to make the most impactful metaphor. That's because sometimes the impact of a single word has a lot to do with its semantic density, what it actually represents in our brain. The example I gave you guys was, "Time is money." That's a three-word metaphor. Yes, time is money, but there's a whole metaphor in there about wasting time and being successful and doing things.

Chapter three: Kathleen La Valle

There's a whole lot of stuff packed into it. And you guys came up with some great metaphors in two words, even one.

Kay: Yes, I think mine was 'time bomb'.

Kathleen: That's right. Another approach is to use situations from the past that were difficult to solve. So if you see a team going down the wrong path in a business meeting and you refer to the 'XYZ project', everybody's going to go, "Oh wait, no, we're not going there!" Sometimes it's that simple; it's an anchor.

But really what we're talking about is the semantic density of these words, things like the phonological ambiguities. So take the word 'check'. It could be a written check of money. It could be to check something. It could be a check mark, or to check on something. You can pick better words that not only run to multiple places in the brain, but to more exciting places. Say I gave you lunch and said to you, "How's your lunch?" And you said, "Oh, it was good, very tasty." That would be a meaning on one level. Now if you used a deeper word, like "it was delectable, it was salivating, it was…" and you start describing things in richer, denser words, it's pulling out more information.

If I asked you what you had for lunch four Tuesdays ago, it's not going to be easy to grab that piece of information unless you eat the same thing every Tuesday. But if I asked what you ate the last time you were at a big party or event, you might say: "Oh it was amazing. We had these little pieces of chicken in this satay sauce, and some wonderful fish with almonds." And when I ask you when this was, you might say it was two years ago at your friend's wedding. So I'm like, you can tell me what you ate two years ago and not what you ate four weeks ago? Why is that? And it's because the semantic density of the meal from that wedding was attached

Chapter three: Kathleen La Valle

inside the brain to more places. The feelings that were going on, the music, the sounds, the relationships, the friendships; everything around that meal was plugged into more places in the brain, and into deeper, richer places in the brain. Then we can pick words that are denser. Even the simple difference between it tasted "good" and it was "delicious." "Delicious" has different submodalities than "good," and when you look at those submodalities, that's the path to increasing things. Because when you start working with people, say you want to take somebody through a threshold, you need to know what are the drivers, especially the critical drivers that push things to increase. So when you start talking to someone and you pay attention and listen and watch how they react when they use certain words, then by using different words and watching the reaction, you can see if you're pushing things bigger or smaller without having to say, "Can you make the picture bigger? Can you make it closer?" So the semantic density of the words that we use also have an impact in that respect of the commonalities in the brain.

Kay: Asking questions like that brings so much more information into awareness, doesn't it? It really helps people to open up their thinking.

Kathleen: Absolutely. As I said earlier, all of this is content-related or context-related. There are times when you want to narrow somebody down. Say they're trying to write a book and they're off in the blue sky somewhere and haven't thought about anything in focus. They wonder why they look at a blank piece of paper and can't begin, and it's because the blue sky of the book's done. That's when you want to pull in and get down to specifics.

Then there are times when you want to expand and push

Chapter three: Kathleen La Valle

beyond. In any interaction with any person, whether it's a client, a customer, a group, you need to have your goal up front; you need to have your purpose. Like it says in Richard Bandler's book, *Thinking on Purpose*, you need to have a purpose before you walk into a room with a group of students, before you walk into a business meeting. You need to know what your purpose is because otherwise you're randomly throwing things out. There are times you want to chunk down, there times you want to chunk up, there are times you want to think laterally. You have to have purpose to know what you're going to do.

> *"The feelings, the music, the sounds, the relationships, everything was plugged into more places in the brain"*

Kay: Something I often ask myself, and I invite my clients to ask themselves, is what is the purpose of what I'm about to say, what is the purpose of what I'm about to do? And that clarity can bring great insights. It feels like cleaning up, vacuuming the brain.

Kathleen: Well, sometimes you have to clean the attic of cobwebs.

Kay: Which is another great metaphor… Recently, I did an interview with Richard, and running through it was the metaphor of how we keep our minds in order during this time. The most important thing we teach people right now is to wash their hands, take personal hygiene very seriously, wear a face covering. And it comes back to personal hygiene within our brains.

Chapter three: Kathleen La Valle

Kathleen: And it's great that a lot of people find comfort in that hand-washing ritual. At least they know they're doing something; they know they can wash their hands, and someone's taken the time to explain how to do it properly. The ritual is where the help comes in, because people are having a lot of fear and anxiety, they aren't doing the things they normally do. They've been taken out of their environment; out of their get on the bus, get on the train, go to work, come home. Now they're home all the time. And people have been getting stir crazy, people have been getting depressed. The key we talked about last time we spoke was creativity, because that's a blessing. People are still complaining about having free time, and there's a whole universe of things they could be doing. I love the museums that were doing virtual tours. I saw museums I never thought I would see. This comes from an attitude; we have to get people to the point where they realise that you don't have to feel a certain way, you don't have to feel trapped because you're in your house, you don't have to feel bad because you can't go to a bar and have a drink.

When I was first in NLP Practitioner training, I didn't know you could choose how you feel, and I was floored when I heard that. I always thought your emotions were something that just happened based on something else that happened. It was a completely alien concept to me that I could choose how I would feel in a situation. And people still don't know this.

Kay: And it can be a bit scary when you discover it for the first time, because you have to step up and take responsibility for the way you choose to feel.

Kathleen: Well, when I first heard it, I was a kid in a candy shop, I was so excited. It didn't scare me at all.

Chapter three: Kathleen La Valle

Kay: I think that's because by the time people come to train as an NLP Practitioner, they're already beginning to open up those gates. I'm thinking about the magical language of NLP and in particular, how playful you are when teaching the Meta Model. Each time I see you teach it, I learn something new; there's a firecracker in my brain for this magical interaction with language.

Kathleen: There are wonderful NLP techniques you can learn, and they're important, but for me the real magic of NLP is in the language. Take some NLP technique which you think always works, until the first time it doesn't. And guaranteed it will not work at some point because a technique is put together from general information, and you don't work with general people, you work with specific clients. So the technique is only a guideline that works with most people. What makes the difference is the language. That works all the time because the magic is in the language. When you're with a client, the first thing you're going to do is listen to their language for what's there and what's not. That helps you in terms of guiding your own purpose, in terms of how you're going to be helping them.

If you're going to do a technique, if you don't use the right language, it has less chance of success. It reminds me of when we do sales trainings in companies. You watch a salesperson, having given them all these great skills, and then you watch them do a role play in a sales scenario and take it right up to the point where they customer's going to sign. And then in one sentence, a pin is stuck in the balloon and it blows up because they use a different presupposition or a different command without realising it because they don't have all the skills yet.

And a lot of people, once we do sales training for them, want to do an NLP Practitioner course because they want the language

Chapter three: Kathleen La Valle

base. The real magic of NLP is when you understand the language models and how to use them. Richard Bandler says this is why somebody will take an NLP technique, do it with somebody and it works great, and a week later it falls apart, or a month later, or six months later – because they haven't built the whole model for them. They haven't built the whole process. They missed things that were being said because they weren't listening to the language, or they didn't install the language.

When we look at the Meta Model at Practitioner level, I always give the trainees experience of the patterns first, rather than just throwing labels out there, because I want them to build a passion for the model; I want them to build a passion for the language patterns. When I first did my NLP Practitioner training, I was scared to death because the trainer said we'd better remember all these labels because they're so important. And then later, the first time I learned it from Richard, I fell in love with the Meta Model. All the scary, spiky things were taken away and at last I knew what it was for.

> *"The first thing you're going to do is listen to the language for what's there and what's not. That helps you in terms of guiding your own purpose in how you're helping them"*

When somebody is really good at NLP, they're using the models, listening to the models, watching the models, and they know how

Chapter three: Kathleen La Valle

to use it because it's the magic, it's the cement, it's the glue, it's the glitter. It's everything else that surrounds the techniques.

Most times when I work with a client, I never do a technique. I might start a swish pattern or a timeline and end up with a collapsing anchor or something else. You know what to use by listening to the client and how they're representing their model at that moment. That's why it's so important that you have the language patterns down.

Kay: That reminds me of my first NLP Practitioner course, which was all about the techniques. I got the personal change I was looking for, so that was great, but I came away frightened. I don't have linear patterning in my brain easily, so it threw me back inside my head, thinking all the time, "What do I do next? What do I do next? What do I do next…?" rather than being present on the outside.

The gift of freedom came the first time I trained with Richard and John and realised it was all about the art and skill of putting things together rather than following a technique. That was such a revelation.

Kathleen: This is the way the brain works. This is the way it develops from childhood. And it's a progression that makes sense neurologically, radiologically. People say, "Oh, my internal dialogue…" It's another thing they think they can't control. Well, your internal dialogue is your programming. It's you running your brain. How you do it, the tone of voice you're using, the words you choose, even how you model yourself.

One time in a training, my husband John had everybody write out their internal dialogue; everything they were saying to themselves in their heads. Then he had them partner up and Meta

Chapter three: Kathleen La Valle

Model each other's internal dialogue. So they asked questions and looked at the pattern of the deletions, distortions, generalisations, and it was a great exercise because people don't realise that it's not just the tone of voice and the volume and the location that's important, but also the patterns you're using inside your own internal dialogue.

They discovered how you can make that more useful, how you can set it in a direction to the things you want to accomplish. And if you're doing things to yourself, like deleting things that need to be recovered, over-generalising or under-generalising, then it's a great exercise to sit and write out everything in your internal dialogue. Of course at the beginning you'll be like, "I can't believe I'm sitting here and writing out my dialogue..." But you'll eventually give that up and just start writing what goes on in your head. Then you'll go back and look and ask, "If that was a client saying that to you, what would you say? What questions would you want to ask?"

To me, the Meta Model is a recovery process, a discovery process. These are just patterns that help you to understand where somebody is focusing and where their purpose lies in the things they're saying to themselves. And sometimes their purpose does lie in the things they're saying to themselves. And you have to find out, uncover the truth in there.

Say you're working with a client and you know where they want to go, and there are certain things they're saying that don't line up with that. And certain things are missing, and that gives you a clue as to where you're going to have to take them.

Distortion is my favourite pattern in the Meta Model because it's the pattern of creativity. The point of creativity is that you can look at something and distort it. Here in the States, we have a TV show called *Flea Market Flip*. You know a flea market, where people

Chapter three: Kathleen La Valle

sell their old fallen apart stuff really cheap? I love that because people say it's junk, and the distortion is the ability to take things and transform them. That's creativity in transformation and it's magical.

Kay: As you were speaking, I was remembering somebody I worked with who had a sort of OCD, if you want to give it a label. We discussed the topic of tenacity and the client said, "I have no tenacity, no determination at all." And I was like, "Well, you can be pretty determined to whatever it is you do repeatedly." And that's seeing what's there that they can't yet.

Kathleen: And for her, the definition of tenacity was very limited. It's so important to really listen to what your client is saying and understand the pattern, not just the content. We have to go beyond the content and go to the process. And help is all about the process, not the content.

Kay: That's such an important message; they're just brain patterns. Some are rigid and others flow.

Kathleen: And the beliefs and values that you're building at the same time, that stuff's draining away – what are you building? People don't know this stuff. Everyone needs to learn how it works.

I had a chance to work with a child who was brain-damaged. I was a teenager about 14-15 years old, and they showed us things to do for patterning. They would take the baby and move the arms, the legs, and turn the head. And they would put peanut butter on his tongue and other things to stimulate the brain from the outside, to get the body to do things. And he improved over the years. It was amazing. By the time I stopped volunteering, he

Chapter three: Kathleen La Valle

was actually talking. He couldn't walk unaided, but he could if you held his hands, because of all this external stimulation to re-pattern his brain.

Kay: It's amazing to me, when you go into a school for children with profound needs, the amazing sensory stimulation they have. It's awesome, and I think why aren't other kids having that? Why do you have to be in that category to be able to activate and stimulate all those sensory channels?

One of my kids, who's grown up now, had a range of labels including dyspraxia when he was young. At the time, Sting, the musician, had a child of a similar age who also had that label and apparently it was cured by a brush stimulation. I remember reading this, and I was keen to do everything we could, so we did the physio, we did the occupational therapy, we did everything we possibly could. But I couldn't quite understand at the time how stimulating the skin with a brush could work. Of course, now I think we missed a trick because I didn't understand how it worked. And we know so much now about neurology.

Kathleen: There's so much coming out from neuroscience now, and we need it. This is stuff Richard's been saying for 50 years, and now the world's catching up. I find it kind of nice that they're catching up finally, even in psychology.

You know, the idea about psychologists hating NLP wasn't true; they flocked to Richard because they were frustrated with not being able to do things. They would bring Richard clients and be amazed. And now there's a whole branch in psychology – Cognitive Behavioural Therapy – and the field of neuroscience is mind-blowing, and these are the things Richard has been teaching for 50 years.

Chapter three: Kathleen La Valle

I read the neuroscience journals and articles coming out now and it really helps to stimulate the things I'm working on the next time because I'm constantly trying to change things up.

Kay: Yes, science catches up eventually. It's fascinating that, for example, we now know how herbs that have been used to treat ailments for thousands of years can affect brain signals. And now science is like, oh, maybe there's something in this thing that's been around for 2,000 years.

You mentioned that you're always interested in finding out more and creating new ways to develop models within NLP, and this an attitude for all of us as NLPers.

"It's so important to really listen to what [someone] is saying and understand the patterns, not just the content"

Kathleen: People notice that when we're running seminars and Richard is teaching, John and I are always in the room, listening to what Richard's doing. People say, "You don't have to be here," and I'm like, "Oh, I'm not missing anything," you know?

People ask me how many NLP Practitioner programmes I've sat through, and I say thousands. Then they ask if I get tired of hearing it, and I'm like, no, it's different every time.

When I got my Practitioner, I was like brand shiny new, but I didn't really feel confident with what I had learned. And every time I sit in on a Practitioner training, I get another nuance, another shift, another paradigm, another angle, another idea.

Chapter three: Kathleen La Valle

Have you seen that movie *Airplane*? I think I've seen it about eight times. And every time I've asked people I know have seen it more than once, they go, "Yeah, and did you notice anything the second or third or fourth or fifth time you saw it? It's so weird, like the first time I saw it. And then it was like the second time it was a joke about the microwave range or something, because I never got that until I saw it the second or third time." Then somebody else will go, "I saw that movie five times and I'm still seeing stuff in the background, or the ambiguities they're doing, the jokes they're doing." Every time you watch it, you see something else. And each time you finish a Practitioner course, you're at a whole different level. Your filters have changed. You're at a different level of beliefs and values. You have different sorting patterns, you have different experiences to bounce things off. So when people ask why would I want to repeat a Practitioner course, I say you'd be surprised what you pick up.

Kay: Every time I come to one of the trainings, I start a new notebook, so I have a big pile of notebooks now. I think I learn something new when I look back through those notebooks. I see the patterns repeating themselves, and see that I just got an 'Aha' on day two. I might see that I'd made a note about it, but I wasn't ready to feel it. And talking about doodles, because I'm a doodler, when I look at some of those doodles, they're each like a metaphor. I remember everything about that learning in that moment which is all captured in that doodle.

Kathleen: There's magic in that. Like I'm saying, teach people the model and give them the experience of each pattern first before I tell them what the pattern is. I won't tell them the label of it. And I make sure they're having a good time, so they're anchored

Chapter three: Kathleen La Valle

to the pattern in a fun way, and they've already experienced it when you tell them the title.

If I started off going, "Okay, so the next thing we're going to do is simple deletions…" in their heads they'd be going, "Oh, simple deletions. What's that? Is that like a deletion? Is it more than one deletion? But it's simple?" Or they'd jump on to what they think it means and then you try to explain it and it doesn't work.

So for me, the ability to give people the experience of the patterns first means they feel that they have the connection to it. And then I make it so obvious when I give them the title that they laugh, and they're laughing when I'm putting it up on the chart. And now it makes sense and they're anchored.

So it's just these are the ways that we help people, whether we're coaching with them or training them or teaching them. It's about giving them the experience first so that it makes sense.

And then I tell them afterwards, try these patterns. You know, even if you just did 10 of each a day. If you really want to be ambitious, do 20, 15, 100. But even if you just wrote out 10 a day of each of the Meta Model, that wouldn't take that long. And because the more you do it, installing it in the three systems, then you'll start generating them, you'll start hearing them more, you'll start being able to use them easily. And it makes everything else that you're going to do with your client, easy.

Kay: It reminds me of teenagers who are looking to learn the curriculum in easier ways. Just bringing in those three systems of learning is often all they need for a lightbulb moment.

Kathleen: Funny story. I was in college, in pre-med at the time, and we had a huge workload, so you're doing things like physical chemistry, analytical chemistry, embryology, calculus, physics, all

Chapter three: Kathleen La Valle

in one semester. And we got to this final, and we were having such trouble; we had to remember the Krebs Cycle, which is the whole cycle of production of energy for the cells. Basically digestion for the cells.

And we couldn't get it, and now there's six of us studying and it's 3am. And we sat up with our notebooks and coloured markers, straws and some cups and things and built an amusement park that represented the Krebs Cycle. And of course we were punchy as hell because we had hadn't slept for two days. And we built this amusement park and everybody in the group all of a sudden immediately understood it. It was like, holy cow. And it was a very complex process with the molecules and transformations and catalysts and everything having to go into process. And we had it down to where we flip over this pen, flip over in this cup, tip this over into that, and the catalyst is this. And we had this entire amusement park built, and none of us had an issue with that final the next day. And none of us could have explained it to you five minutes before we did this because we were so confused about it.

So sometimes it takes doing something like that to make it fun, to make it unusual, make it different. This isn't something any of our professors would have told us. As human beings, we have that creativity.

Kay: What a great example of learning made easy, which of course is how little children do it so effortlessly. One of the great things about social media is that you can watch all those little videos of children just learning whatever it is they're doing. They're fully immersed in their kinaesthetic bodily experience. I love it.

Kathleen: And people always ask me if it's difficult to work with children. Working with adults is difficult compared to children.

Chapter three: Kathleen La Valle

Children are much easier to work with in NLP because they are still in that playful learning, and they don't question as much as adults who have all these belief systems and things built up.

You can say to a child, "Okay, now take that feeling in your stomach and make it pink and fuzzy and let it tickle your stomach instead of making your stomach hurt." You say that to an adult and they'll look at you like, what? You know, take the picture and give it like purple lights, and an adult would be like, "Does it have to be purple? What if I wanted blue lights? Can I put the lights in the picture?" With a child, you could tell them to make the picture bigger, take the picture down, push the picture away. Adults will question it and say, "I'm not sure I'm moving it fast enough, am I moving fast enough?" Children don't do that, they just go for it and so it's easier to work with them because they have that wonderful ability to play.

"These are the ways we help people, whether we're coaching with them or training them"

Kay: I so agree. The children themselves are a precious gift and I love the way they just absorb new things. It's their supporting systems that so often need help, and I'm forever managing the beliefs and values of the parents, teachers, siblings, aunts and uncles...

I once worked with a child who came up with a wonderful idea about having a unicorn stop her nightmares. She came up with it all by herself; the unicorn's horn was going to stab the nightmares, so they would disintegrate. Then the parent said, "Well, I think you should sleep with Mummy anyway, just in case the nightmares come back…" presupposing the child's own solution wouldn't work. Hence the need for educating the parents.

Kathleen: When I teach the Master Practitioner programme, I do a process with the delegates to bring them back to the wonder of childhood. Part of what we do in NLP is teach adults how to go back to that magical thinking, that child thinking. I always say, I have to get old, but I don't have to grow up…

www.purenlp.com

Chapter three: Kathleen La Valle

Chapter four: Joy A Thorne

JOY A THORNE

Joy A Thorne is an NLP trainer, coach, and assistant on many of Dr Richard Bandler's courses. I met Joy on a Shamanic training more than a decade ago and love her nature-based approach to spirituality and human development. Joy lives in the UK's beautiful New Forest where horses roam freely – a metaphor perhaps for this wise woman. We recorded this interview early in the 2020 lockdown, when I asked her how she was managing her home environment and mindset, and applying practical skills to the business of thriving.

Chapter four: Joy A Thorne

Kay: Joy, we're in lockdown, and what better time than now to be able to spend some time finding out how different people are managing their wellbeing. I wonder what helps you and those living with you to thrive?

Joy: Well, we're very fortunate because we live in the New Forest, so we can go out, we can go walking and cycling, and enjoy the sunshine. So on a physical level, we're doing that, and we're enjoying home cooking, we've got a lot of food and we have people delivering organic vegetables and fruit and things like this. So we make lots of healthy meals and we're keeping tummies full.

We're keeping our spirits high by looking at what's going on, questioning things, seeing whether we agree or disagree with the policies that are being brought out and discussing that.

Kay: So, thinking about the physical environment, this is a time for many people to explore new perspectives about how they arrange their physical environment and create structures, boundaries and zones, especially those who are new to working from home.

I'm particularly keen to focus on what we can do in a covert way to help others in our environment to be well. For example, atomising essential oils, burning herbs or having the windows open and letting some sunshine in.

I know you're very attuned to the more natural ways, and as you say, you live in the beautiful New Forest. So if you could choose one power tool for helping your environment to feel energetically vibrant, what would that be?

Joy: Well, it depends where you live. Where I live, I can open the doors, let the sunshine in and let the wind blow through the house and keep it in the flow of energy. One of the things I also find really wonderful is to vaporise. Clove oil gives a really special feel to everything so I often have that burning.

The other thing is spring cleaning and sorting through the house. And if you've got a garden, getting out in the garden, and giving a sense of order to the chaos is really good for our minds.

And going back to the mind, because you know the physical, mental and emotional all seem to be of the same matrix from my perspective, I'm taking a very holistic approach to the whole thing and making sure people can at least feel positive, have a laugh and maybe watch something funny on the TV. I think that's an important thing as well. Though I'd say don't watch too much of the doom and gloom. You know you've only got to watch 10 minutes of news to get the vibe of what they're telling us next. After that, I might have a think about it, but it's not something that needs to be kept going over in our minds. The situation is as the situation is at the moment. So get practical in the house, keep organised, clean up, take the time to develop a functioning system, because it's good for our mind and body.

"When you feel the collaborative energy, it raises the soul, it draws in great spirit"

Kay: And there's something in what you're saying about a perception of control – we like to feel that we are in control of our environments. While our thoughts and feelings drive behaviours, our action, even if it's mundane doing, gives a really positive message to the mind and body. You mentioned earlier opening the doors and windows and letting that air flow through. That reminds

Chapter four: Joy A Thorne

me of so many of our eastern philosophies that have existed for thousands of years, like feng shui, for example, which says let the energies pass through, or stop them if you need to, so having some choice around that. I was thinking that the other day when we did that big collective doorstep clap for the NHS.

Joy: Yes, it's uplifting for everybody to feel that collective energy. Unification and collaboration feel very special.

Kay: And that's brought connection within neighbourhoods. You could hear the resounding clapping throughout the neighbourhoods in my town, and I'm told throughout the UK. And there was something really dispersing about the action, dispersing the energies. And regardless of anybody's beliefs, these simple practices have been around for thousands of years.

Joy: Yes, group consciousness is so powerful. And when we learn to utilise group consciousness accurately, I think we stand a chance of being able to transform much of what happens on our beautiful planet Earth. I know that might sound a bit 'out there' to some people, but from my perspective, when you feel the collaborative energy, like everybody was feeling the other night, when clapping together, it raises the soul, it draws in great spirit. Everybody feels the connection to that which we are. And that raising of the vibration is one of the healthiest things you can do at the moment.

Kay: I think this is a time for us to come through with a better collective consciousness and more powerful self-awareness of our own innate healing capabilities. You know, we're being forced to look at how we as individuals can keep ourselves in a healthy state; opening our minds, rebalancing, being aware of the messages we

Chapter four: Joy A Thorne

give out to others and which we can choose whether or not we receive from them. And I think your point about watching TV or listening to the news is such an important one. If you can keep some distance and choose what you allow in to shift your emotional state, if you have that power, that's great. Do more of it and improve it. And if you don't yet, then there are some simple ways of being able to manage whatever is coming in from the outside, staying unaffected by it or dispersing it very quickly.

Joy: I think the first place to start is knowing that you're allowed to choose what you focus on. That's a freedom. That's a birthright. Then we've got to do some housekeeping and tidy up what we allow into our minds and what we don't allow into our minds, what we look at, what we focus on. Of course, we need to know what's going on in the world, and then we need some tools to manage our own mental and emotional states.

I mean, the amount of people I encounter suffering from anxiety before all of this happened, it seriously makes me wonder how are they managing at the moment? I'm talking to quite a few of my clients at the moment and they're managing okay because I'm talking with them, but there is a need for people to really understand that they, as adults, have some say about what we tune into and entertain in our minds.

Kay: That reminds me of the work of Richard Bandler, who talks about thinking on purpose, being clear in your awareness. Noticing if you're habitually watching television absorbed by the news, or whether you're watching with purpose to filter for something useful. So knowing the difference between habitual focus of attention and deliberate focus of attention. It's a big shift for many people.

Chapter four: Joy A Thorne

Joy: It is a big shift for many people. We're always going on about how everybody's addicted to their phones. But if I tell you that all you've got to do 24/7 is look at your phone, you're going to get bored of it. That's human nature. This situation could be a way of getting people bored, and it raises the potential for people to put their phones down, do something else and move. So in that sense, that's a good thing.

Kay: Which leads me to my next question perfectly, which is now that you have time, more time than perhaps you had before, perhaps the demand on our time is less. What I've noticed is that a lot of people I'm in contact with are learning something new or doing something new, picking up a habit or an old activity. Is this something that you're choosing to do because of this lockdown?

Joy: I'm choosing to speak to more people for free, I'm choosing to say what I really think more openly, because I'm normally a little bit closed and I only speak to those people I know really connect to my sort of thinking. So I'm talking with people I wouldn't normally be talking to, often helping them get into a useful frame of mind; and that that's a big thing at the moment because some people are getting a bit wobbly. So I'm going to be doing far more of that than I do normally because I'm offering shifting out of anxiety help for free to those that can't afford it in these unprecedented times.

Kay: People reaching out and helping others, offering services for free, is something I'm hearing so much of, particularly in our community. I think we're hearing the call to help because we have a skill set that can be of enormous value right now in the world. And helping people to navigate the weeks ahead, the months ahead, maybe even longer seems to be really important to us.

Chapter four: Joy A Thorne

Joy: The other thing I'm doing, which I don't necessarily advise everybody to do unless you've got the gumption for it, is to really look at lots of different points of view on what's happening at the moment. And you know, my opinion on it at the moment is, do what the official guidance says, but question everything. And look deeper if that's useful for you, though there's no need to look as there are plenty of people looking. There are plenty of people saying a different narrative to the one we're being given through the media. And I think it's okay for people to look at that if it satisfies something in there. And it's interesting. I don't think that's for everybody, but it's worth knowing that it's going on

Kay: And you know, our brains love a problem to solve; something we can aim our cognitive skills towards.

Joy: Yes to doing that, as long as it's not concerning people and making them run off into, "Oh my God, my God." Because 'oh my God' is not a great state to be in, but it's good to show the world that we're just going to take a little time about this to see what's actually going on.

Kay: I think it feels like we have more time each day, even though as you rightly say, we don't. But it feels that we have the time to stop and check in with ourselves, check in with our nearest and dearest and make new decisions about how we spend our moments.

One of the things I hear quite a lot from my clients and social networks is that people are doing things in the home that they perhaps didn't do as much of before, like meditation and qigong, tai chi, yoga and so on. Because increasingly, getting out and about is difficult for many people, although you and I both live on

Chapter four: Joy A Thorne

doorstep of woodland so we're very lucky. So if in three minutes you could give one simple instruction to somebody who's listening to this who needs to just stop, centre and ground, what would be your go-to piece of advice?

Joy: Yes, but before I do, I just want to say something about something I saw the other day which made me think on this subject. It was Russell Brand, I believe, interviewing Wim Hof, the Dutch motivational speaker and extreme athlete known for his ability to withstand freezing temperatures. Russell was asking him how he was able to climb Mount Kilimanjaro in shorts, run a half marathon above the Arctic Circle barefoot, and stand in a bowl of ice cubes for more than 112 minutes, among other incredible and almost inhuman achievements. He asked how he got to be able to survive so easily, and do things like go into a laboratory and be injected with bacteria, and have the scientists watch his blood destroy the bacteria.

Wim Hof has taught thousands of other people, so it's something our bodies can learn to do. But one of the things he was talking about was this breathing technique, which is a very deep breathing technique that you can find online if you're keen on jumping

---

"Running off into 'Oh, my God...' is not a great state to be in, but it's good to show the world that we're just going to take a little time about this to see what's actually going on"

Chapter four: Joy A Thorne

into icebergs and things. I think he shocks his body to go right back down into the spaces of the reptilian brain. The body is just the pulse and the heartbeat and the breath; all the automatic functioning of the body, with nothing more than the living energy field emanating from the body.

And I was thinking, you know, that's similar to a state I do and teach people in certain meditations for healing and rejuvenating. One of the ways I access this is sitting still and focusing down the midline of your body. It's like using our minds to search inside, tuning into invisible geometry and pivotal points of balancing.

Gravity always passes through your body; no matter what position you're in, you've still got the midline. To get into that space and bounce around the midline and then let your awareness just to drop with gravity down through all the different tissues of your body and everything, while allowing all of the normal functioning of the body just to continue, breathe naturally, don't interfere with each breath that we breathe, just notice where we feel the softness, where we feel we are relaxing and allow that feeling to sort of resonate from the centre, going out to a periphery. And I like the idea of this periphery being like a personal spherical space, with you suspended in the centre. You know, the distance to the edge of your personal sphere when somebody comes up to you and gets in too close and they've pushed up against the edge of your periphery.

I call this accessing your sphere of joy. It's so good to be able to really tune into it and feel that sense of gravity going through every fibre of your physical body and then feel the feeling of gravity filling the spaces between the atoms that make up your physical body, just allowing your body to feel its solidity within the sphere. Tune into the rhythms and the pulses that you sense within your physical body within your personal sphere and keep breathing natural.

Chapter four: Joy A Thorne

To me, this sort of meditation generates a nice, grounded feeling. Feeling the weight within our centred bodies is a wonderful way to start accessing the ability of a body to be able to restore itself, helping to boost the immune system and allow healing to take place. And that's a place to go now, with all what's going on out there at the moment. Take some time to be still in the moment. Open up and drop inside it, and it's yours, it's your birthright to be able to tune in to that which is good for you. Do it just because you can.

Kay: That's fabulous Joy, thank you so much. I really enjoyed that practice; a super way to hack your autonomic nervous system and focus entirely on the parasympathetic nervous system. Stay well, stay healthy and do whatever you need to do to be bring more Joy to the world.

www.joyangelthorn.co.uk

Chapter five: Dr Mark Chambers

DR MARK CHAMBERS

Mark Chambers is a friend and colleague I've known for around 12 years, and I deeply admire his commitment to continual learning of new approaches to holistic health. Mark is a retired GP who now consults, coaches, and teaches as an Integrated Healthcare Practitioner and Generative Coach, and he is the author of the book, *A Bedside Manner*. This conversation was recorded when the world was in lockdown, at a time when each morning Mark ran free mindfulness sessions online. In this conversation, Mark references so many inspirational people and themes of our times, and reveals the true nature of taking the Hippocratic Oath.

Chapter five: Dr Mark Chambers

Kay: Mark, you and I seem to be interested in the same things in terms of wellbeing, and you're teaching me mindfulness at the moment. What would you say would be the big chunk of your interest?

Mark: I'm interested in helping people to help themselves to feel better. Essentially, that's my elevator pitch, that's what I do. I was a GP for 38 years, and since I retired from General Practice three years ago, I've been running a coaching and clinical hypnosis practice, which keeps me busy. I've also been doing quite a lot of teaching. I've been teaching hypnosis to doctors and medical staff, and teaching mindfulness to anybody who wants to learn. That's been the big thing for me for about 15 years now. I was introduced to mindfulness by Dr. Stephen Gilligan and got curious about it mainly because patients were talking about it, so I thought I'd find out what it was about. It features a lot in the way I approach my work now.

Kay: And mindfulness is a word I think a lot of people use easily and they think they know what it is. How would you describe it?

Mark: A very fair question. My interest came from patients who were coming back for mindfulness treatment with emotional and psychological issues, having previously been referred elsewhere by various practitioners. What they were describing were mindfulness-based interventions of various sorts, with some mindfulness as part of the process, but also psycho-education. They were describing a lot of cognitive content exercises and things to be doing with their thinking mind.

So I looked into this, guided by one of my colleagues, an osteopath, who was very interested. He introduced me to the

Chapter five: Dr Mark Chambers

person who introduced me to NLP. He said, "If you want to know about mindfulness, then go and read Thích Nhất Hạnh's work. He's the Vietnamese Buddhist monk who wrote the book, *The Miracle of Mindfulness*. Soon after the Vietnam War, he was exiled to France and this was a little pamphlet of instruction sent back to his people in Saigon who were struggling without him. It's a very short, simple booklet; a simple instruction, essentially. His definition of mindfulness was, in five words – the practice of conscious awareness.

I teach a mindfulness programme with a colleague, Jenny Thornton, and that's essentially the basis of it. It's just helping people, noting and letting go of all the cognitive content in the moment and coming back to this awareness of the practice of conscious awareness. So it's a practice. It's something we do. And the thing that we do is consciously pay attention, without any content. So it's like having our brain or our awareness go out like a radio, just having it switched on but not actually tuned into a station. So just being in the present, in a state of equanimity. Nothing to respond to, nothing to react to, just being awake and aware in a non-reactive way.

> *"I don't regard mindfulness as a therapeutic intervention. It's not a treatment; it's a skill. It's an ability that is part of our natural human condition, which is really where I started becoming interested"*

Chapter five: Dr Mark Chambers

Kay: So how do you handle an enquiry like, "Well, what's in this mindfulness stuff for me? How does it work?"

Mark: I don't get many enquiries like that; they're usually fairly indirect. People come to see me because either I was their doctor for many years, or they know someone who knows me. I get a lot of referrals from former colleagues or consultants for people who aren't responding to a standard western medical approach because there are other things going on.

I don't regard mindfulness as a therapeutic intervention. It's not a treatment; it's a skill. It's an ability that is part of our natural human condition, which is really where I started becoming interested, because it's not a therapeutic thing.

Some 40 years ago, John Kabat-Zinn and his colleagues in Boston, Massachusetts developed Mindfulness-Based Stress Reduction. More recently, Mark Williams and his colleagues in Oxford have developed Mindfulness-Based Cognitive Therapy. These techniques have proved very helpful in therapeutic contexts. They use an understanding of mindfulness as a way of getting people into the starting blocks and then add content, therapeutic interventions, onto this.

So some people do come because they know I teach mindfulness and become curious about that specifically. People come because they've been labelled with an illness or had some sort of psychological or emotional label attached to them, and usually they aren't particularly bothered about the particular approach we're going to use. They just come with an expectation and a hope and some motivation that in some way we're going to find a way forward for them. It's a sort of refuge of the diagnostically and therapeutically destitute; people who have had the western-type labels attached to them, often with psychosomatic complaints.

Chapter five: Dr Mark Chambers

Things like irritable bowel syndrome, fibromyalgia, chronic fatigue. These are very definitely symptomatic, unpleasant conditions. People have all sorts of different stuff going on for them. They're aware they have unpleasant feelings. They are dis-eased. Western medicine hasn't found a specific disease, there isn't a pharmacological approach to alter physiology or a lump or something to chop out or remove. There's no active, external thing that can be done to help them.

So my interest in mindfulness is in helping them to access what they already have; the resources they have, what they need. It goes back to Hippocrates; the Hippocratic Oath and using the natural forces within us that are the true healers of dis-ease. The problem is that thinking gets in the way, so we have to still the mind to stop this. Then what we seek can emerge.

Kay: There's something about that just stilling and opening up, isn't there? One of our NLP presuppositions is that the resources a person needs are within them. But do you find, as I certainly do, that there are a lot of people who don't believe that? They don't believe that the healing is within them, and the resources are within them. They believe that the responsibility for their wellbeing is with their GP, or with a medicine, or it's somebody's fault or solution or whatever.

Sometimes I find that a lot of it is in just leading them towards an experience of feeling good, when you can expand the inner worlds and find new resources. Do you recognise that sort of process?

Mark: The thoughts going through my mind in response to what you have asked there is that I think most of the work, if work it is, is in the preparation. It's getting people to that place where

Chapter five: Dr Mark Chambers

they're ready to start to make some change, because the work is about change. People come because they don't feel right, they're not right, but they don't know what to do. If they knew what to do, they would go away and get on and do it.

They come when dissociations become intolerable to them. The "I want that, but this is happening."

Dr Milton Erickson's work has had a great influence on my career, and he said that the dis-ease occurs when the conscious and unconscious mind have lost rapport with each other; the body being the unconscious mind, the conscious mind being the things I want. I think one of the great problems with the western approach to psychotherapy is that it pathologises these processes, sees them as 'diseases'. Stuff is happening within the individual that is dis-integrating, taking these parts apart, and rather than working as a coherent whole or asking what resources we have, it's seen as a disease and something that needs to be pathologised and treated.

I think I'm probably going off on a bit of a tangent here, but the whole work is preparation. You know Socrates says, "When the student is ready, the master appears."

I don't regard what I do as treatment. I don't market myself as a therapist. You know, as in the original meaning of the Latin word 'docēre', I teach. A doctor is a teacher. So my job, or our job, is creating the environment, the place where people can come in safety into a nurturing, supportive environment; where they can do the learning. It's a bit like midwifery, if you like. Something is trying to emerge, and just allowing that process to take place so that the symptoms can transform and resolve.

The unconscious mind doesn't have a voice. It can't talk. It can't say, "I want this," or "I need that." So it talks in symptoms of emotions. And if you don't listen enough, it talks with lumps and bumps and all the rest of it. Until we take notice and start

Chapter five: Dr Mark Chambers

saying, "Okay, what's this trying to teach me?" Or, "What am I supposed to be learning from this?" and create a welcoming place of curiosity where we can allow our creativity to engage and let something develop and emerge.

So if people come and they want change-work, there are three basic essentials that need to be present. They need to know what they want, so we spend a lot of time clarifying, in NLP terms, well-formed outcomes. They need to have some clear idea, because almost all the time they'll say, "I don't want to feel like this anymore." That's fine, but when you know what you want to feel like, then we've got something to work towards and we can start doing some useful stuff together. So they need to know what they want. They need to take responsibility for it. I can't do anything for them other than help them towards the goal or goals they identified for themselves that are consistent with their values and congruent for them.

> *"You just need to be set up to give a gentle nudge to help [people] to step into the unknown a little bit and embrace their fear of failure"*

And it has to be now. A few weeks ago I had someone come and see me. I send people a questionnaire before we start, and she'd filled that in very sketchily. Usually, my experience is that the more detail people put in their preparation questionnaire, the better outcome they get. So if it's a, "Yes, no, yes, no, I want to stop smoking, yes, no..." I'll do whatever you tell me, kind of thing,

Chapter five: Dr Mark Chambers

we're probably not going to get very far.

Anyway, there was this woman who wanted to stop smoking. She came in and she said, "Well, I'm ready."

"What do you mean, you're ready?" I said.

"Don't you remember me?" she said.

"Well, I remember," I said, "you contacted me a few weeks ago. I sent you a questionnaire and you sent me some pretty straightforward answers."

"No, no," she said. "I came to see you as a patient ten years ago, asking if you could help me to stop smoking, and I asked, 'Can you stop me smoking?' and you said, "No, nor can anybody. But when you're ready, I can help you." Then she said, "So, I'm ready now."

The thing that takes the time is getting people to that threshold, and when they're ready you just need to be set up to give a gentle nudge to help them step into the unknown a little bit and embrace their fear of failure; get them into a place where they're not afraid of failing. Instead, they're not afraid of failing enough. And we have to go ahead and create a safe landing place for them, so that if things don't work out, they're not abandoned.

A fundamental problem with western psychotherapy is this idea that, "I'm okay. You've got the problem..." And there's some pathologising going on and isolating them. Psychopathology is the study of isolation, and that's the great problem I saw with the way I was trained to treat emotional and psychological issues, as though they were problems. You know, I even slipped into the language there, which is information that the unconscious is desperately seeking to communicate.

Kay: I completely share your views and that's certainly my experience too. There's something about the whole alignment process of a self-holistic wellbeing that is a simple but very powerful

Chapter five: Dr Mark Chambers

director for us. And your point about education is bang-on. That's how I view every single interaction; it's an opportunity for me to help somebody to learn something more about themselves. Whether they know it today or tomorrow isn't so important, it's just connecting them in.

And so coming back to the mindfulness, the conscious awareness, the practice of conscious awareness, what would you say for you has been the most profound ability or exercise in conscious awareness that you've discovered, you've practised, and you're not letting go of it under any circumstance?

Mark: The skill that emerges from it is this ability just to stop and become aware, from a slightly dispassionate place, a slightly dis-associated place, of what's going on. This ability to just create a little bit of space, so that we can respond rather than react when stuff happens.

When we become stressed, we default to our level of training, not to our level of expertise. We just default pretty much immediately, instantaneously to some dissociative pattern. And almost while we're still doing it, I know I'm going to say, "I wish I could stop myself. Why am I doing this?"

People say. "I want to lose weight, but every time I go into the kitchen I open the fridge and have another piece of pork pie and then say, 'Why did I do that?' I promised myself I wouldn't do it today, etc, etc." Just allowing that little bit of space to stop and just become aware…the practice of conscious awareness…the way we do this, we do this by paying attention to our breathing. So this is bringing the mind back into the body.

So to empty the conscious mind, we give it a job to bring attention to the breathing and become aware of it. In the training, especially when people are starting, we spend a lot of time repeating this over and over again. Just as soon as thoughts come into awareness within the meditation practice, we notice them, let them go and bring awareness back to the body doing the breathing.

There are a lot of myths about mindfulness. One is that you have to meditate. There's Mindfulness Meditation, but you don't have to practise it to be mindful. You don't have to meditate. Meditation, in my understanding, is simply the process of coming back to centre; media = centre, middle. It's the process of coming back to the middle of the body. So it's a good idea to do this, but you don't need to do formal meditation.

You can use every breath as an opportunity to become aware of that, and just come back to centre and just be aware of where it is coming in and out and where we're feeling it in the body. So coming out of the head and into the body, that's the simplest exercise, the simplest bit you can do. And as soon as you've done that, it creates that little bit of space: "Okay, here I am about to go off on one…so stop, take a breath, just become aware where it is. Okay, what is it that was bothering me?" Then, even better, you can just kind of float out into a clean, third place and say, "Ah, there's Mark feeling a bit upset about something."

Then there's the Ericksonian mantra – "That's interesting… Something's waking up; I'm sure that makes sense. Welcome." Finding the safe holding place with equanimity and clarity, you can start to look at what's going on and then step back in and observe. And having taken note of what's going on, form some options, step back in and engage, and take some action appropriate to what's going on. So just increasing that space between stimulus and response. The old psychological model of cause and effect is a bogus idea nowadays. I think it's only psychology and social sciences that still think in terms of cause and effect.

Since Niels Bohr and Max Planck invented quantum physics 100

Chapter five: Dr Mark Chambers

years or so ago, we have been able to become aware that we live in this world, this quantum universe, of infinite possibility. So stimulus and response happens. With this approach, we're just seeking to put that little bit of space between stimulus and response. So when the trigger comes, instead of just defaulting into the dissociated reaction, we just put that little bit of space in and this allows us to bring our awareness to choosing our response.

Essentially, we have little or no control about what happens to us and in our environment, but we do have choice about our response, but only if and when we put some space in there between stimulus and response.

Viktor Frankl, the concentration camp survivor, said the only freedom you can't take away from a person is their freedom to choose how they're going to respond. And if we just leave it to our unconscious conditioned patterning, we'll go down the same old route time and time again. As soon as we come up with a bit of a gap in there, even if it is one breath's worth, and say, "Okay, I've got a choice now. I can go down the old path or I can explore doing things differently."

It needs curiosity and being prepared to fail and all the rest of it. By putting in that gap between stimulus and response we have more than one way of responding. We have choice. When we react, we have no choice. So that's a useful thing. Just noting, so when stuff happens just to stop, take a breath, and just recognise and acknowledge, accept and then just let it go. We don't need to engage with it. It's just a thought. It's just a feeling. It's just an emotion. It's just an idea. It's just an image, you know; neurological activity in the brain. Just note and accept it.

That doesn't mean passively giving in to it. Just in the moment, that's what's happening. This is where we are. Now we can ask ourselves how we can most creatively engage with this and turn

Chapter five: Dr Mark Chambers

any obstacles and challenges into resources.

Kay: And I guess at that point, you talk about choice; when people perceive they have a choice, then they open up their future and can find new ways to get to new places. But when people don't perceive they have a choice, even though we know it's there, they don't perceive they have a choice. And you mentioned Viktor Frankl as a really good example. In a concentration camp, he still found the ability to have a choice. What do you think is the key obstacle in people's ability to perceive choice?

> *"We have little or no control about what happens to us and our environment, but we do have choice about our response"*

Mark: Good question. The obvious answer that comes to me is awareness, or lack of awareness. Which is a kind of circular discussion. It brings us back to the same point; once we find awareness of this lack of choices, there's potentially possibly a conditioned response, just something we keep telling ourselves. And if we keep acting and behaving often enough, then it becomes almost a self-fulfilling prophecy.

But to Frankl, the only freedom we have is this ability to choose, and we all have that; it's just not being aware of it. As you say, it's the blinkering. So helping people to find this bit of space so they can become aware.

People usually, in my experience, feel they have no control over

Chapter five: Dr Mark Chambers

what's going on, which of course is true. The Sword of Damocles – we have very little control over anything. And that's what brings most people to us. Either people are trying to control them and they don't like it, or they're trying to control other people who don't want to be controlled, and they don't like that either.

So I think helping to get rid of this notion of control and realising that that's a choice that's being taken at an unconscious level. And that's the point about these choices not being conscious choices very often. It's getting people out of their head and back in touch with these parts of themselves that they will never understand or be able to have a cognitive-type conversation with. Just an awareness that whatever is happening, a choice is being made.

I remember when I was learning psychology, the term 'secondary gain' kept creeping in. You know, these people are never going to get better because they've got a secondary gain, as though they're consciously deciding, "I'm going to get my migraines every weekend, so I don't have to look after the kids all weekend," and all the rest of it.

They don't take that conscious decision, you know? They work hard all week without a migraine. The old weekend calls, when the GPs used to do weekends on-duty, often on a Saturday morning there would be a visit request for someone with a migraine or similar. "I can't get out of bed," and all the rest of it. But by Monday, whatever we did, they were back at work and okay and coping again. And so it was said to be all secondary gain.

In my way of thinking, there's no such thing as a secondary gain; it's just a primary gain at an unconscious level. It's that whichever part is driving the bus and making the decisions and choice at that point is the bit that is much more powerful. Take the idea of the horse and the rider. You know, the horse is saying, "Well, we're

Chapter five: Dr Mark Chambers

going that way. It doesn't matter what the rider wants, it's going to happen." That's where this choice is happening. There are all these different ego states now. In Ego States Theory, there are perhaps 150 different ego states in play at any one time and they're all jockeying to be the one driving the bus. And depending on which one actually gets hold of the wheel and gets to do it, is what happens. When this is all conditioned in, it's all happening below the level of consciousness.

Kay: You've used some lovely metaphors there, like driving the bus, the horse and the rider and so on. Metaphors help us to understand a bit more about ourselves, don't they? And you know, I always picture those electro-chemical communications in our neural pathways going, "Oh, we always go this way…so let's do it again." And we do it again and we do it again, until it's become autopilot. And it's that autopilot you're talking about, isn't it? So you do an and/or debate, and if you don't bring your awareness into it, you'll just continue to do what you always did.

Mark: And the unconscious is lazy. It's a slightly pejorative term, but if it does something and it worked once, and it does it again and it works another time, then the more often it seems to get a result, it'll just default to it. If we had to learn something anew every time we encountered it, we'd never get anything done.

We need to put some patterning in there so we can get on with life, otherwise we'd never be able to do up a shoe or get out of a room. We'd have to go onto Google to work out how to open a door every time we came up to a brass knob in front of us. Once we've learned that's the way things work, we store the pattern away in automatic pilot and crack on with life.

So I think these are parts of our natural programming. And one

Chapter five: Dr Mark Chambers

of the skills is to utilise this stuff, to know that we have this ability to learn useful stuff. But also that we need to know when to unlearn the stuff when it becomes redundant, and learn better stuff.

The metaphor I often use when people come to see me is a mobile phone. Most people have a fancy smartphone, and after about three months, the little light comes on showing 'software update available'. And they think, "Oh dear, I'm not going to press that. I won't be able to use it for a quarter of an hour." So you leave it. And three months later there's another one. And if you leave it two or three times, it becomes pretty useless because all the software you want to run, the operating system can't cope with it anymore. There's nothing wrong with the phone; it's just running old software, which when it was installed was exactly the right stuff, but it's obsolete and redundant now.

So what you need to do is have the courage to press the update button and go and make yourself a cup of tea for 10 minutes, then come back and the phone's working perfectly because it's no longer running redundant software.

Kay: That's a good analogy. And Mark, you mentioned dissociation. I know from other conversations I've had with you that you're very clear about there being a difference for you between dissociation and disassociation, whereas I use them interchangeably. And I'm really interested to learn what for you is the difference between those two things.

Mark: Well, dissociation, this is my learning… Actually, what I should have prefaced all this with is that you should be aware that, after getting my name right and a bit about my biography and history, nothing I say after that is true. The question you should be asking yourself is whether it's useful or not.

Chapter five: Dr Mark Chambers

So there was a French psychologist and psychologist in the second half of the 19th Century called Pierre Janet, and he coined the two terms 'rapport', which we use now, and 'dissociation', a French word. And he used dissociation to mean the parts which are completely out of conscious awareness and conscious access; the stuff that kicks in, and we have no conscious access to it whatsoever.

Conventional western-trained psychiatrists would be comfortable with the concept of dissociation. Freud trained with Janet and used this model of dissociation. His idea of repression is that the unconscious mind takes things that are so difficult and so unfathomable and so impossible to face to a place outside of conscious access. They're still there and they're still very powerful and they're providing very important drivers. These are unconscious conditioned patterns that we dissociate to. So if we drop something, we shout, we get stressed without thinking about why we didn't need to do that. This is an automatic, dissociated part reacting. If we're able just to put a pause in, we can create a gap between stimulus and response, and this gives us the

"These are parts of our natural programming. And one of the skills is to utilise this stuff, to know that we have this ability to learn useful stuff. But also that we need to know when to unlearn the stuff when it becomes redundant and learn better stuff"

Chapter five: Dr Mark Chambers

opportunity to have some choice in how we respond. In contrast, dis-association describes a process that can be a conscious activity. Like I described with the ability in mindfulness practice to take yourself consciously to a place where you can observe with a degree of dis-passion. Bessel van der Kolk, a psychiatrist who has specialised in the management of psychological trauma for many years, describes the 'watchtower' – a safely distanced psychological place where we can take ourselves and sit and observe in safety. You know, the thing I was describing earlier of feeling a bit anxious – fluttering in my chest, anxiety, feeling anxious – then just going out into a place and saying, "Oh, there's Mark feeling anxious."

You know, this is a conscious thing. I dissociate into anxiety. Something happens; the anxiety comes from within me. This dissociated part took over the wheel. The disassociation is the bit that, when I become aware of the feelings and symptoms of anxiety, I can then dis-associate and look from this watchtower – this safe place.

Hilgard, in his hypnosis teaching, talks of the Hidden Observer. When people are going into hypnosis, there's a part of them that knows they're being hypnotised, so they've still got a foot in both camps. You know, enjoying the journey of hypnosis, but still knowing they're a part of it. There's an unhelpful idea prevalent in people who are not trained in hypnosis that someone in hypnosis is under someone else's control. It's not my understanding of what hypnosis is about at all. There is always this Hidden Observer, the part of us that is in touch with reality, whatever that is. As 'Professor' Robin Williams said: "Reality. Now there's an interesting concept…"

When we're hypnotised there is also a part of us that knows that we're doing some sort of responding to what the agent of change is eliciting.

Chapter five: Dr Mark Chambers

Kay: Yes, I love that. You mentioned hypnosis several times and you've already made the distinction between mindfulness and meditation, so where does hypnosis sit if we're doing a contrast between those three terms?

Mark: Good question. So hypnosis, mindfulness... and what was the third term?

Kay: Meditation.

Mark: Meditation... Well, my understanding – and again, nothing that I say is true but may be useful – meditation, media, centre, is the process of coming back to centre. So if mindfulness is the practice of conscious awareness, then meditation would be training in awareness. So it's a practice we do.

Usually, meditation practices involve some kind of physical thing, relaxing the body in some way, and a mental thing, like giving the mind a focus, something to do, essentially emptying the mind and just giving it one thing to be focused on. So it could be an image or a thought or meditating on an idea or concept, or it could be a mantra, which is usually a word or an expression. In mindfulness meditation, we use breathing as the focus, just bringing the awareness to the breathing. So that's kind of the three components of that. There are as many different definitions of hypnosis as there are people offering definitions of hypnosis. In the postgraduate diploma in Medical Hypnosis that I did, the definition is about two pages long. There's a person, a hypnotist, another person or the subject or subjects and the hypnotist does things to change the experience or the belief or memory of blah, blah... And so it goes on.

The best definition, the one I like because it's the one I made

Chapter five: Dr Mark Chambers

up, is that hypnosis is the artful use of communication to alter neurology. So it's becoming aware of what's going on and then using communication to elicit a change in state. So you could be using spoken language or a facial expression like raising an eyelid to elicit a change, to get a response. If I raise an eyelid, and the person I'm communicating with raises an eyelid back to me, then that's a bit of their neurological state that has changed. So some hypnotic phenomenon, some hypnotic interaction, is taking place there. But more specifically, it's around learning. It's helping someone again with this question about choice, taking people to a place where they have a choice.

In professional practice, my favourite definition of hypnosis comes from the teaching of Dr Milton Erickson, the psychiatrist who played a huge part in bringing hypnosis back into clinical practice half a century ago. He described hypnosis as, "The elicitation and utilisation of unconscious learning to meet the needs, values, competencies and interests of the present self."

And in terms of intention, when I think of using these things in a clinical setting, the purpose of mindfulness, the whole point about mindfulness, is there is no intention. You practise mindfulness to practise mindfulness, stilling the mind so that what you seek can emerge.

So with hypnosis there is an intention – you know you're coming for hypnosis to stop smoking, to have some control over your weight, your eating or whatever – so there's a purpose and intention in hypnotic practice and the techniques that might be used. The point about mindfulness is that it's content-free. All this work is about state, and the single most important factor in getting any outcome we want is our state. And our state is entirely the product of two things. It's about our practices. So it's important to have practice, a daily practice to get us into resourceful states.

Chapter five: Dr Mark Chambers

The other thing about our state is that it is a consequence of where we are placing our focus. So putting our focus into the present moment, getting ourself into a resourceful place, making compassionate connection to self in the moment. And then the mindful state is content-free. There's nothing going on; it's content-free, subtle, non-dual, non-reactive awareness.

The non-dual aspect is that we are active participants in the creation of our own experience. Subject and object are the same thing. So the mindfulness state is content-free, subtle, non-dual, non-judgemental awareness spread uniformly everywhere. Within us and through us and through space, every part of us, and we're a tiny atom in a vast, an infinite, universe. At the same time, the whole of the universe is flowing through us. So we have access through this state to this huge quantum field of infinite possibilities and resources. So we create this space within and around ourself where we can hold the problem, the unmet need, but also hold all the resources it requires. Because they are all there. Everything we need is already there in this space.

The other thing I'd like to add, having said that, and banging on about Dr Erickson, is that definitions of hypnosis often refer to suggestion and the acceptance of suggestion. So Richard Bach, the author of *Jonathan Livingston Seagull*, describes hypnosis as the unconscious acceptance of suggestion, which is a nice picture of the classical hypnotist-subject type stuff. Erickson developed a second-generation of hypnosis. He certainly used suggestion techniques, but there was a much greater depth to his work than this, in the elicitation and utilisation of unconscious learning, which is central to the ethical application of these techniques. So getting back to this idea that we have all the resources we need; the intuition, the learning is there, and our jobs as the agent of change are to elicit this and create an environment for healing – healing being the Greek word for health – the whole environment.

In this environment, the conscious and unconscious mind can link and start dancing and making music together: a cooperative model. So Erickson was very much about eliciting this unconscious learning that was in there, rather than Freud's view of the unconscious mind as this rather lurid place with dark desires and evil spirits floating around. Erickson regarded the unconscious as this huge repository of vast learning and experience; not just of our own experience, but of our genes bringing us all the experience of 13.5 billion years of evolution. It's all in there. Just finding and getting access to this beautiful place.

Kay: I like to invite my clients to explore the potential they were born with, and I often use the metaphor of arriving as pure stardust; bright, shiny light that somehow we forget is there. And actually if we could just allow it to come through… Sometimes, we have to clear some space to reveal it, as you point out.

And so in this current time of lockdown, there's been so much

> *"The unconscious [is] this huge repository of vast learning and experience; not just of our own experience, but of our genes bringing us all the experience of 13.5 billion years of evolution. It's all in there"*

Chapter five: Dr Mark Chambers

collective contribution to supporting people's wellbeing through Zoominars, all sorts of online platforms, and this general sense that we need to work at being resilient.

For some people, they were already resilient, so it's just, "Hey, I can get even better at this." While for others it's, "Oh, I've got this time to do wonderful things with it." But some people have found it a quite a distressing time because they've previously lived their life at 1,000 miles an hour, super-busy, and then suddenly the world goes bang. It's a perfect opportunity for them to become consciously aware of themselves. Do you think there's this sort of fear of self-discovery?

Mark: That's a good question. I can't say that I've ever come across that as a fear that people have openly expressed that they're afraid of what might emerge, what might come from them. There is certainly fear manifesting at the moment, and my coaching business has been as busy as ever in this period. As a doctor, I work for a medical charity providing a resource to doctors who are struggling, who don't want to be labelled as ill or whatever, and that's the reason they choose to come to coaching rather than to therapy or intervention.

So this super-doctor stuff… we don't get ill and all the rest of it… but there's a lot of fear. It's generally fear that brings people to ask for help. And their coping ability to deal with that fear comes… Well, I'm not aware of it being fear of what might be emerging from them, but rather this uncertain unknown future. Particularly doctors on the front line who are particularly at risk of getting this horrible virus, just questioning whether what they're doing is really… Well, they're perhaps questioning their vocation a little bit sometimes, and how they could be better at using and applying their time.

Chapter five: Dr Mark Chambers

So it's not my experience that people are afraid of what might emerge, but that they tend to come in – and this is possibly just the way I'm working, the stuff I'm doing – the ones who know there can be more, part of them is telling them there can be more to life than there actually is for them. And they're wondering how to actualise and to realise that, and bring it out.

You've raised resilience, and if I can just say a word or two about that, I've been working with doctors for two or three years since I retired, essentially through the College of Medicine, looking to set up programmes to help build resilience. Burnout is a big issue in medicine, and resilience is the word that tends to get used and is becoming somewhat unpopular really, because it's like mindfulness and all these other things that have been around, and you get bored so you have to find something else to say. And I think the notion, the model that's emerging, which I find helpful, is the idea of psychological preparedness. So rather than resilience as a protection and something that needs to be there, it's just building up from within the strengths and abilities to deal with what's going on. That's the kind of model that seems to be emerging.

My particular interest is in emotional and psychological medicine. In this field, pretty much all the terms, all the diagnoses, come from physics and the physical sciences. Stress is an example of that. Stress is the term used when a force is applied to a system. Resilience is described in terms of the response of the system to this stress. I think one of the ways to help people is to start taking the emotion out of these descriptive terms and become curious about what they mean. In science, the resilience of the material is the amount of external force or internal force (stress) that the material can absorb without suffering permanent deformity.

I think that a really important and useful aspect of this metaphor for the psychological concept of stress is that it is something we feel.

Chapter five: Dr Mark Chambers

When we become aware of stress building, we can learn to spot when enough is enough and walk away. This ability to walk away at the right time is a key skill in building resilience. When we have restored ourselves, we can step back in and tackle a bit more. In this way, we can learn to observe our experience and response form a place of equanimity and thus build up the strength and resources to cope, be flexible, and adjust appropriately.

This is getting back to the mindfulness stuff, where you can just observe and watch the onset of this awareness, being honestly aware with yourself of what's going on, saying enough is enough and being able to meet experience with a smile. This ability to smile tells us that mind and body are communicating. You know, we've got to be able to smile and do what we do seriously with great humour.

Once we have this awareness, we can bring a full skill set into play. In the caring professions, we need to bring compassion and tenderness; compassion to feel people's pain and suffering and to want to do something about it, and tenderness to do this kindly and gently. Before we start with other people, we need to bring these skills into our relationship with ourselves. This essential kindness and compassion is not enough on its own. If that is all we have, we're soon going to be to be crushed and overwhelmed by the load. So there needs to be an element of warrior spirit and the determination that goes with it. The warrior in us brings strength, fortitude, grounding, and armour to shield us Another part of the warrior is a good bullshit detector. So to know when something genuine needs to be done, and when a slightly tougher approach might be necessary.

A third component of the attribute set we need is a good sense of humour and the playfulness that goes with it. You know, this creative, playful approach to things; as if every situation is new.

Chapter five: Dr Mark Chambers

How can we make this into an adventure and challenge these obstacles? How can we turn them into resources and let them present their gift to us? That to me is what resilience is about.

We are thinking beings. We have a cognitive mind. It does the thinking. It enables us to cognitively approach stuff, give meaning to our experience and then also find some self-efficacy to say, "Okay, this is what I make of it and this is what I'm going to do to help me deal with it when the going gets too tough. This is where I keep the smile and bail out." Because whoever fights and runs away lives to fight another day, and that's a key resilience strength; to know when enough is enough and to have these daily personal habits. So you're building up and building up and building up, reducing stress and building resources in daily activities. This is absolutely key.

This is for ourself and for our environment. So this is where we were before this all kicked in, and everything has been derailed over the last couple of months. I encourage the idea of the canary in the coal mine. Self-awareness: people checking in with themselves regularly and spotting early when they're getting into difficulty. Helping people to develop and practise daily habits of taking care of themselves and preparing themselves. For me, it's teaching them mindfulness. There's yoga classes, there's going for a swim, there's playing an instrument. For some, it might be prayer. Short, regular practices every day that briefly allow relaxation and release from responsibility. These are best if they're pleasurable and perhaps gently challenging. They're best when there is resonance and musicality, as this builds the mind-body harmony. This is the essence of mindfulness practice: emptying the mind and bringing awareness back into the body. With practise, one breath can be enough to do this. There's doing whatever people want to do for themselves to refill their barrels. Virginia Satir used to describe

Chapter five: Dr Mark Chambers

the barrel, or how you can't pour from an empty jug. These are useful metaphors.

You have to be looking after yourself, building resources, reducing stress where possible. Addressing both the canary and the coal mine. As well as working on ourselves, we also have to introduce systemic changes in the working environment to reduce stress and the environment made a more friendly and appropriate place to work.

There was a very good paper by the GMC [General Medical Council] a few months ago that identified three really important items as ABC:

A is autonomy, the ability to choose, so people know that at every point they have choice, and when enough is enough, they choose to walk away. "I can usefully do no more. I need to go and recharge".

B is belonging. We're a social animal. Resilience is not something we can do on our own. We need other people, we need contact. We need our Communion of Saints around us. Zoom has been a great blessing in this. This applies not necessarily just to people. We have access to through nature and spirituality to the mystery and beauty of life. Regularly immersing in this with gratitude is another vital and essential aspect of our daily practices. I remember Golda Meir, the Israeli prime minister, who was in her own very isolated place since the 1960s, the Yom Kippur War, 1967 or so. And years ago I watched her being interviewed and they asked her, when she needed a bit of help or advice, who did she go to for help? And she said, "There are two people I always ask when I need guidance. I speak to my grandma and I speak to my granddaughter." They said, "Oh, what do they say to you?" And she said, "Well, they can't say anything. My grandmother has been dead for 20 years and my granddaughter hasn't been born yet. But I'll ask them both what they would want me to do."

Chapter five: Dr Mark Chambers

So you have this sense of belonging, and communities are important to us. Just now, people are dying and their loved ones can't be with them, they can't hold their hand. And we're a social animal, we need other people. But they are there for us, just like in the Golda Meir example. She knew the importance of accessing her Communion of Saints.

C is competence. Essentially, there are two aspects to competence. Internal and external. There is having the skills and the ability to do the things that we need for ourselves. There is also an external component; we need the opportunity and ability to use the skills we have out in our world. One of my fears in the current situation has been the hold-up of PPE equipment. People know how to help others, but they have been put into this dangerous position where they do not have access to the right equipment to enable them to do the things they need to do in safety. In many situations, people are choosing to do what they can anyway and putting themselves at increased risk.

The concept of 'moral injury' has emerged. I think it's a really useful frame; the emotional and psychological consequences of knowing that if only you had the resources available, you would be able to practise professionally in the way you were trained to do. When this all blows over – and hopefully it will blow over and we'll come out of it the other end – I think there'll be a lot of emotional and psychological morbidity in carers because they will know they could have done stuff if only they'd been given the equipment and the materials they needed to do it in the best possible way. So there's this idea of moral injury, the consequences of knowing you could do something, but are unable to do so for reasons beyond your control.

So, ABC – Autonomy, Belonging, being part of something bigger, and Competence, of having the skill set yourself and also

Chapter five: Dr Mark Chambers

being enabled by your environment to do the things that are important for you to do, which includes walking away,

Kay: That's really powerful, Mark. As you were talking about that, the pictures in my mind were connecting to nature, because nature teaches us about resilience. And you know, if a storm comes then the soft bendy tree manages to bring itself back up afterwards. And the oak tree, sometimes the stress is sudden, and it shifts, and the tree falls over. But I was also thinking about those artificially grown plants in poly tunnels that are given artificial supports. And as soon as they're asked to support themselves – like you buy a little herb plant or something and you bring it home and suddenly it's out of its environment. And then it dies because it hasn't learned to respond to new environments. I think this is a metaphor for our times; that we should always, even back to the very beginning of time, be preparing ourselves neurologically, psychologically, physiologically for what is to come so that we've got more choices at each door along the way.

Mark: Yes, it's all about state now, the COACH state: Centred,

"When this blows over...I think there'll be a lot of emotional and psychological morbidity in carers because they will know they could have done stuff if only they'd been given the equipment and the materials they needed"

Chapter five: Dr Mark Chambers

Open (i.e., content free, just flowing through), Aware, Connected to resources, and creating a Holding place, so we can welcome the resources we need as they flow through. And there's a place for them to embed and grow and help us.

In our problems, we can CRASH. That's Constricted, Reactive, Analysis paralysis, Separated from resources, Hurt and Hurting. It is this CRASH state and the inability to resolve it to COACH for themselves that brings people to us.

And back to the Buddhist ideas that have advised mindfulness… There are some myths around mindfulness; that you have to meditate, say, which you don't. You don't have to be silent. And you don't have to be Buddhist. But certainly silence helps a lot. That's what we're aiming for. But you can be just doing the washing up and be aware of the temperature of the water, the texture of the soapiness and all the rest of it. You can meditate in those moments, just be with it.

John Kabat-Zinn, one of the great mindfulness teachers, said that to say mindfulness is Buddhist is much like saying that gravity is English because Isaac Newton described it. It's a human attribute; the Buddhists have just taken it on and produced a really useful set of instructions and guides as to how to mindfully meditate very well.

Kay: A term I use with my students is 'bandwidth'. The bandwidth of your sensory channels and how at any one time your thoughts can overload your bandwidth, so you can't process your experiences so accurately through your senses.

And my take on mindfulness, for what it's worth, is that it's an opportunity to clean up. It's rather like a computer defrag, so that we make space to better handle the information we're processing in any one moment.

Chapter five: Dr Mark Chambers

Mark: It's just a thought.

Kay: It's just a thought, yes. It's just a thought.

Mark: Or we could wake up, lighten up, step up; be here now and notice. And then allow cognitive diffusion: "It is just a thought." It's just a feeling. It's just emotion. In this moment. I can just let it go. Maybe I can re-engage with it at another time, but at the moment, it's just a thought, just a feeling. Let it go. So what's important to me? Re-align with my values. So what am I going to do to take action in-line with my values? So I see the way I can take mindfulness into a useful way of being.

You asked earlier, what's a useful thing? Okay, so wake up, lighten up, step up, be here now and notice; notice what's going on. It's your thinking, your feeling, whatever. Okay, it's an emotion, it's a thought, it's an idea. It's intention, so just for the moment, let it go. And then okay, you've done that little bit of practice. You have let go and come back to the moment. Then what's important to me? My values… so take action based on that. Do stuff. Speculation is always in the doing.

Kay: You have the phrase, don't you, that it's not learned until it's felt in the bones?

Mark: It's from Papua New Guinea – nothing is learned until it's felt in the bones. The body keeps the score. Eugene Gendlin's research demonstrated that if you're working with people in a coaching environment, the single most important indicator that they're going to achieve the outcome that they claim is the outcome they want is that they can get a felt sense of what it is.

So there you are, in hypnotic language, you future-pace, you get them to hallucinate what it's going to be like when they've achieved the congruent change that they've identified they want. That's got to feel good. So you have them dis-associate, push that back into the future and come on back here. So that's what you're headed for – a nice, dis-associated image, using the language correctly.

Kay: I've written it down! I'm on it! So there are a couple of things I just want to tidy up. One is that you have a book, a lovely book, at least one that I know of, which is *A Bedside Manner*.

Mark: Yes, it was published about two years ago. So this is what I taught doctors for 25 years about consultation skills, essentially. And this is really the stuff we've been talking about. It's not what to do, it's much more about how to do it. It's all about state and all the things we've been discussing, like motivation and rapport. And it's everything I learned in 38 years as a GP. It's a good book for the loo; you can get through it in three or four visits.

> *"My favourite definition of experience is what you get when you don't get what you want. So hopefully people can get some vicarious experience from this"*

I mentioned Hippocrates earlier, and one of the parts of the Hippocratic Oath is when we get towards the end of our career, one of the things that's expected of us is we start giving stuff back; all the useful things we've learned. My favourite definition of experience is what you get when you don't get what you want. So hopefully people can get some vicarious experience from this.

Remember, nothing I say is true; the question is to ask yourself is whether it's useful. And if you found stuff that's useful here, then take it, make it yours and absorb it and use it in ways that are right and appropriate and work for you.

As I approach the foothills of senility and wander off more and more to the golf course, those of you who are picking up the baton can hopefully use some of the things that took me a while to learn and absorb them for yourselves.

www.collegeofmedicine.org.uk/mind-body-faculty

LOUIE B FREE

Louie B Free is the host of Brain Food from the Heartland, The Louie b. Free Radio Show, broadcasting from 21 WFMJ. Since early 2020, I have made several appearances on Louie's US radio show and absolutely love his warm, generous style of interviewing. Louie is a wonderful example of how candid conversations can offer something to every listener and how everyone has an interesting tale to tell. In this interview recorded in early 2021, Louie and I reflect on ways of dealing with trauma and explore the necessity for connection.

Chapter six: Louie B Free

Louie: Ladies and gentlemen, This is the Louie B Free radio show with Brain Food from the Heartland. I'm so thrilled and honoured to have Kay Cooke back with us today. So Kay, just for the new listeners out there, tell us a little about yourself.

Kay: I live in the UK, where I was born and bred and I live in the north of England, close to the Scottish border where, like most of the world, we're in lockdown right now. What I do for a living is mind coaching, brain training. I've got a background in education, health promotion, sport and all sorts of other things and I'm just on a mission to help the world think more intelligently, behave with more purpose and manage emotional states better.

Louie: I'm going to ask you about lockdown over there. I don't want to compare and contrast, but people are really complaining about things here. I mean, we're really in lockdown.

Kay: Well, we're not supposed to connect with anybody outside our own household bubble and we have no contact with the outside world unless it's essential; essential work, essential healthcare, education. I think we come out of this lockdown next week and then we'll see what our government says is to happen next.

Louie: How's it been for you?

Kay: Well for me, it's been pretty straightforward. It's given me a chance to focus in on the things I want to focus on. For example, I've been looking at the developments I want to make in my own business and with my team. And it's given me no excuse to go out and find other things to do. So it's a fulfilling time. I have a lot of work with my clients online and it's very important to me to do

Chapter six: Louie B Free

what I do, to help other people. There are lots of good things to come out of lockdown. The difficult things, of course, are the fact I'm desperate to see my children and give them hugs. They're all grown up, they all live elsewhere, so I'm desperate to see them and other family members. Just that connection with friends and being spontaneous.

Louie: Hugs.

Kay: Hugs, yes.

Louie: You know, I'm glad you mentioned that. You know that TV show called *Friday Night Dinner*? Well the first episode showed the wife trying to get the husband to get rid of his *New Scientist* magazine collection. And my wife said, "That's you, the new scientist," because it's my favourite magazine. If I've got a project that I need to get done and my *New Scientist* comes in the mail my wife won't tell me that it arrived. To be really honest, she'll hide it from me because I squeal "Oh, my *New Scientist*…!" And then I'm gone. I grab my reading glasses and I'm gone, and I'm totally distracted, regardless of the importance of what I needed to be doing.

   I love it. There's an article in a recent issue about evolution and how it holds the key to why social distancing is so difficult, about hugging and our need to connect. So that's why lockdown has been really, really difficult. And I can't imagine what that's like for you, not to be able to be with family.

Kay: Exactly, we're social creatures. We have a huge part of our brain that's hard-wired to seek connection with other people and that drives a particular neurochemical called oxytocin. I also

Chapter six: Louie B Free

believe connection is a really important function in our evolution. And when that's taken away, it does all sorts of things to our primitive brain that can set off a stress reaction.

What we have to do in these situations is override the instinctive stress by providing a smarter narrative. So you know, instead of fighting the reality of this current isolation – "I'm going into implode or explode because this isn't fair. Why is it happening to me?" – it's better to stop fighting with the universe, with nature, and the natural order of things because you ain't going to win that one.

But what we can do inside our minds is improve thoughts that give us a better chance of adapting and navigating through to whatever is yet to come. There are shortcuts to overcome our current deprivation of contact; ways we can deliberately connect. Your job as a radio presenter keeps people connected to others. And Zoom has become an amazing new friend to many people. Yes, we're not physically touching, but we're still making connections and that helps regulate emotions, despite missing physical touch.

It's suboptimal of course, but we have to adapt. I feel it's

> *"There was an article about evolution and how it holds the key to why social distancing is so difficult, about hugging and our need to connect. So that's why lockdown has been really, really difficult"*

Chapter six: Louie B Free

important that we understand that social contact is a basic human need. Yes, it feels like it's being taken away from us now, but if you fight and scream and shout, then you'll be driving lots of stress chemistry. And why would you do that?

I always say, just take your lessons from nature. You know, a storm comes, the plant falls over. It doesn't get up again and go, "Hey you storm, you F-ing so and so, you shouldn't have done that. You did that on purpose. That's not fair…" No, nature doesn't do that, it just picks itself up and reorganises. But our brains like to make up stories to make sense of the world that we live in.

I don't know if any of that makes absolute sense.

Louie: It makes absolute sense to me.

Kay: You know, to connect to people during these times, we just have to be more creative and find other ways of doing it.

Louie: And again, like you say, with Zoom, Skype, whatever people are doing, is it optimal? No. But it's when I think about what it would have been like had this happened 10 years ago or 20 years ago, when all we had was the phone. Now we're able to connect with people online, as opposed to maybe writing a letter to somebody and hoping that the letter carrier picks it up and gets it there. We're spoilt. We're able to text. I'm able to text you in the UK. And I just think that's incredible. I just have to remember the time of day…

Kay: I know… it was late at night… [laughs]

Louie: I have to remember that. My phone doesn't make a noise because I don't I have it set so text messages buzz. A lot of people

Chapter six: Louie B Free

do, and they've let me know it's 4am and I'm like, "Oh, I'm sorry!" But we do have great ways of communicating,

Kay: Absolutely, and I think the next level of developing this conversation is to explore what we mean by connection, because that means different things to different people. So, what's the purpose of connection? Because again, if you look at the natural order of things, it's a two-way process, and a connection involves some kind of flow state.

And of course, not everybody sees it that way. Some people need what they perceive as connection because they just want to be able to express themselves. Other people want to receive things. We all have different agendas.

We ask questions, we talk, we look at people, there are many levels of communication. We connect ideas, we connect from the heart space, we connect physically. There are lots of ways that we can connect with people and being clear about what your own needs are and matching them with the needs of others, I believe, is very important.

Louie: So let's talk a little bit more about Happy Brain. I just I love it. I've had so many comments from listeners about Happy Brain and I absolutely love your work. Tell us a little bit more about it.

Kay: Thank you, Louie. Well, my work with Happy Brain is, and forgive me if this sounds twee, my life's work. It makes sense of everything I've ever experienced and everything that I believe I can facilitate in the world around me. It's a model I created to help me make the science, the education, the more convoluted and complicated aspects of wellbeing, as simple as possible. So with very simple illustrations, words, case studies, activities, we

Chapter six: Louie B Free

teach people how they can better manage their inside worlds and become more resilient in general.

I work with people of all ages and a whole range of difficulties and problems, and I'm particularly invested in the next generation. I think we've discussed before that when I work therapeutically with older people, they've so often been practising their problems for decades. And I estimate that 90% of those problems could have been prevented had they had a different skill set embedded in early years.

> *"We all get stressed and sometimes that stress is useful, but why hold onto it?"*

We owe it to the next generation to teach them better skills for managing themselves, and they're not doing so well at the moment. I see a generation of kids, particularly teenagers, who've been so lovingly nurtured and cared for and protected by parents who kind of think, "I will not let you have any bad feelings at all. I'm going to make the world change around you. It's not your fault…" and so on. I'm exaggerating to make a point of course; we're all doing the best we can. But there are some basic skills that, if they're put in at the foundational level, have a profound effect on wellbeing and happiness.

Think of a sausage machine. You've got the input end of the raw ingredients and then you've got the output end with a sausage. So often clients come to me as sad sausages; you know, the ingredients early on were either not put in the right sequence or they weren't of the right quality. So if we could reverse-engineer that whole machine and go back to the start and say, "Okay, in a perfect world, which of course doesn't exist, but you know, what would those basic ingredients be?" And it seems to me that we need to change the fundamentals earlier in the process.

Happy Brain, to answer your question, is about three key principles. It's Clarity of the thinking mind, to aim towards something you want. It's Resilience of self-managing emotional states that build rewarding relationships. And it's the Simplicity of influencing the autonomic nervous system and reorganising the inner world as quickly as possible. It's a great introduction to NLP and a specialist application of NLP for people living or working with children and young people.

If you take yogic breathing as an example, like the old wisdoms where grandma might say something like, "Just breathe, dear. Just breathe…" what does that actually mean? And you go [sound of fast breathing] okay, but you can hyperventilate. That's not what's meant. What's meant is a kind of breathing that sends a signal to the brain to say, "You're okay, calm down, you're okay. It's all right." This is breathing that expands the lower lobes of the lungs and connects the vagus nerve through deep rhythmic breathing, focusing on the long out-breath. It's the simplest of ways to begin to bio-hack your own system and such simple mechanisms can have a profound effect.

We all get stressed and sometimes that stress is useful, but why hold onto it? For example, you're walking down the street and a truck careers towards you – your heart races, your adrenaline pumps, everything in your body is preparing you for an alerting, avoidance reaction. Cool, well done body, that's fight or flight – run to get away from the truck, or fight it, which wouldn't be a good idea. And the energy of a survival response that's been created in a nanosecond needs to discharge. Animals go off and shake to release it. What do we need to do? Movement helps, as does deep

Chapter six: Louie B Free

breathing. And your brain records the way you dealt with the danger. And then the stress should dissipate. But what about the people who then go home and start to think, "Oh my God, what if that happens to me again tomorrow? What if..., what if..., what if it happens to my kids, my partner, my friend? Oh, my goodness..."

This time, with no clear and present danger in the outside world, they start the stress reaction all over again, just with a thought. And that isn't smart. Okay, we want to take away a really good lesson to keep you safe from trucks in future, but why recycle the stress? It's not useful and it doesn't have anywhere to go, so it depletes us.

We've got a brilliant survival mechanism, we've got a thrive mechanism and we've got a stress mechanism, but we don't want to live in stress. So my aim is to direct people's attention and skills towards thrive. The survival mechanism has a place and is useful if there's a real danger from the outside world, but the place where we can really build resilience is that middle ground of stress by resolving the inside world into thrive.

Louie: Kay Cooke, I've talked about this a lot in the show, but what I hear is people kind of regurgitating trauma, bringing it back and re-playing it. I've talked about this before on the show; I was sexually abused as a kid. And when I first started to come to terms with that, I was in my twenties and trying to figure out why. I was drug-seeking, in different relationships, promiscuity, and someone suggested that I go to a group called the Help Me Group. And again, I don't want to sound critical, but it was a professional therapist who ran it, and I remember them going around the room and they came to me and said, "Well, tell us your story." And of course, they didn't want to hear the good story; I guess they wanted to hear about why you were there.

I remember going for a few weeks and they came back to me

Chapter six: Louie B Free

and said, "Tell us your story. You know it's safe here." Well, I told her I didn't want to go over it. I didn't want to do it again. And I realised I was feeling worse each time I left there. People would commiserate, which was nice. People would hug, people would cry, and I would feel worse leaving because it wasn't dealing with it. It was just regurgitating it over and over.

I remember I was speaking once at a group – this was way before my radio days – on a panel with psychologists and social workers. And the way I dealt with it was I'd tell jokes about my own abuse, not anybody else's, but about my own. And someone said, "Well, you're laughing about it, but aren't you in fact scarred for life?" And I thought, wow… It made me think of scars that I had from altercations early in life, and I thought well, they fade with age. And I said, "Well, it's not an open wound unless I rip it open." And the way they were talking about it, kind of re-playing that trauma, is to what end? Any traumatic experience, like almost getting crushed by a truck, do you really want to keep re-playing it?

Kay: Wow Louie, that's a huge topic. Dealing with trauma is extremely complex. We need a narrative that helps our mind make sense of what has happened and sometimes the kindest thing you can do is just give yourself a story that allows you to put it away. But the event itself gets encoded in the nervous system, and from a survival point of view that makes sense to your brain, which needs to be super-prepared for any sign of that known threat. PTSD is when the full survival reaction gets triggered out of nowhere, but as I say, the essence of what we are talking about is how life experiences get etched into our neurology.

Our nervous system is constantly patterning electro-chemical signals and favours heavily repeated patterns or those that have been glued in place by intense emotional experience. But we

Chapter six: Louie B Free

can and do have great success in healing trauma, and NLP and hypnosis are brilliant ways of reorganising, re-patterning the neurology. Once you interfere with the neurological pattern, it can't run in the same order again, so the brain can now go to other places.

Of course, it's not that simple for everyone because these things often have layers of complexity, because for some people, through no fault of their own, they've learned to benefit in some way from holding onto the trauma and keeping it present with them. And that's a Pandora's Box…

Louie: I do get what you're saying. I know people who have defined themselves with it and it becomes part of who they are, as opposed to something that happened to them. It's sad when you see that.

> *"There is always an opportunity to re-educate the brain, to give it a better chance of finding a more rewarding way of operating"*

Kay: I think there's always an opportunity to re-educate the brain, to give it a better chance of finding a more rewarding way of operating. When an adult comes to see me with some kind of trauma, they make a decision about healing it, dealing with it and how they want to move forward. If they're not ready to do that, if they want validation of their suffering, I'm not the person to see. If they are ready to do it, we can have fantastic results. The sadness for me comes in when I work with children. Because children, who

Chapter six: Louie B Free

can experience terrible things, as you so candidly share, can also, in the right environment, heal themselves very quickly, because they are very adaptable. However, the parents or the system around them also gets traumatised by children being traumatised, and that's where complexity comes in.

I can think of examples where a parent's whole sense of purpose becomes to crusade against the perpetrator, and then they get chained to their identity benefits. Now when I use the word benefit, it's perhaps not the right word, but If I'm in a coffee group and I've got a story that's going to create a big emotional response in the group around me, that's like someone going to a help group and triggering an emotional response in the people around them. And there's something unhealthy but equally quite compelling about connecting with others in an emotional drama.

And for some people, one way to connect to their own stress is through the distress of others, which starts to grow into a snowball. Like I say, it's not an easy subject and it's a massively deep and complex one.

Louie: So, while we're talking about Happy Brain, if you're giving kids the tools – and obviously we want kids not to experience trauma – if you give them the tools early, it's much easier, correct? If somebody teaches you how to change a tyre, then when you have a blow-out on the road somewhere, you don't have to get the manual out and try to learn it because you remember how to do it. Maybe that's a terrible analogy, but if you give them the tools when they're young, it's going to be much better, hence Happy Brain, correct?

Kay: Absolutely. I feel so very strongly that we need to give the next generation better skills. But this is also a stealth model, which

Chapter six: Louie B Free

is by teaching adults how to teach their children to have better skills, then they themselves have to process that new information inside their minds. And as you rightly said, traumas happen to us all and you'll be surprised at how many people who look very cool, calm and collected on the surface, deep down are struggling. Often, what you're seeing is a successful strategy for coping.

If we scoot along our timelines to the pearly gates, I think in Daoist tradition it says that if we live in the flow, in the Dao, we can live for 120 years, so I always invite people to think about that. So you reach the pearly gates. There you are. You've had 120 years of a wondrous and vibrant life. And you look back seeing the highs and the lows, the left turns and the right turns and all of that stuff. What do you want to feel most satisfied with? What do you want to feel proud of (or whatever the descriptors are that fit you)? How will you know when you've had the most rewarding life? And somewhere in that, I think you find clues about how to lead yourself through the next part of your life. Nature knows how to fall over and adapt, and we need to figure out how to pick ourselves back up and walk again, if possible, in a more rewarding direction.

We are magnificent learning machines. To me, that's what intelligence is; constantly connecting neural pathways in new ways inside our brains. You don't just pick yourself up and then walk back into the same drain every day. That would be stupidity. But people do that.

When you go to the pearly gates and set up a dialogue between your present and future selves, you can ask, "Okay, so in order to have led my most rewarding, satisfying life, what do I need to put in place at this point in time?"

Louie: Beautiful, I just I love how you said that. I also love that on your website you have the Einstein quote, "Humans are only

Chapter six: Louie B Free

limited by the boundary conditions of their thinking." I love what you do for our world Kay. And I want to ask you again, as I know you work with universities, what is that like when you're developing programmes and working with universities? I know you recently did some resilience training in a master's degree programme in social work at Durham University, so when you were doing that, how was it received? I've got to believe that it's a lightbulb thing.

Kay: The big chunk is yes, absolutely. I think the younger version of me as an educator was much more about the curriculum content, hoping to connect my students to the knowledge. These days, I'm much more about finding out where people are at, and then leading them towards the next thing they need to know.

When I work with universities, by the way, I work with staff as well as students, so the agenda may be different. With staff training, or in any corporate situation I'm hired into, like so many other trainers, we're generally hired in by somebody who decides this or that is needed. So that first contact is really about connecting with the group, giving them some quick wins, some quick takeaways so that they can go, "Wow, now I'm interested…"

The one thing that almost all human beings are supremely interested in is themselves, so it's quite easy to run programmes and workshops that help them to learn more about themselves. There's also a big reciprocation because I'm learning something wonderful from them. I get new ideas as I'm learning what's real for them in live time, and I love that. That, for me, is how we all grow.

Louie: I've got to ask where the sense of satisfaction comes from with what you do? You're such a warm, giving and loving lady. In all our communications on and off here, I see you smiling. There are people out there whose ego gets in the way. Not you. Where

Chapter six: Louie B Free

do you think a desire to help, to give, to do the work you're doing, comes from?

Kay: I just truly believe the world can be better than it is. In my early career days, my colleagues used to call me Pollyanna. I believe every human has infinite potential. I believe I have infinite potential. And every day is a great discovery for me, about me. I truly believe that.

> *"I believe we have so much potential, and we're only scratching the surface of it"*

In my early teaching days, I imagined myself as a net coming from underneath my students and bringing them up through the curriculum, so they owned it. And I still believe that so strongly.

Not everybody gets that, and I don't share it that often, but that's the baseline. I truly believe we have so much potential, and we're only scratching the surface of it. You talk about ego and I've learned, you know, when my ego has completely got in the way, or ignorance perhaps, because I've always been a bit bombastic in enthusiasm.

When I worked in health promotion, everybody I came into contact with was bombarded with my latest level of understanding about coronary heart disease. Of course, it came from a good place of total enthusiasm, but it was misplaced. And what I didn't have then was what NLP has taught me, and that's the ability to calibrate and match the level of where somebody is. It's back to the fact that it's a two-way process because you know, I can give you information, I can receive the information, but we will truly grow and evolve if we share it. And that requires us both to be present and responding to each other and really listening.

Before we came on air for this interview, you asked what we should we talk about and I said, "We'll know from moment to moment, because we'll chat in a live and responsive way," and that's what I've learned to add into the enthusiasm. I've tempered it a lot, but it's so frustrating when I see somebody in front of me and I can see this big diamond within them shining, ready to come out, and they can't see it. Yet.

Louie: Because if they're overwhelmed, well, they won't necessarily be ready. If you can see the potential in someone, let's say to train them to do certain physical exercise, you're going to be able to get them to run, walk, hike, whatever, 5 miles, let's say. What you're saying is you've got to meet them where they're at and maybe start by walking. So even though you can see the potential, you've got to meet them where they're at?

Kay: I believe very much so. And I think it's a good analogy.

Louie: I'm so blown away by your ability, your desire, to see the goodness, what the world can be. What people focus on can make them so negative, and you maintain the positivity of looking at people and seeing that diamond. Do you ever wonder? The older I get, the more I wonder. I see where some bad behaviour comes from, but I'm always intrigued by where that sense of heart and wonder comes from in people. Do you ever wonder where that comes from?

Kay: Yes, and that's a whole other conversation, and then we go

Chapter six: Louie B Free

into my beliefs about life, the universe and all sorts of other things like sense of purpose.

Louie: It's a choice you make, correct? Is that what you're saying? That it's a choice?

Kay: I don't know...

Louie: Where do you think it comes from then? I know I'm pushing, but..

Kay: Well, I believe that we have a purpose. And I've always been very clear from my first day at school that I'm an educator. That's what I do. My parents tell a lovely story of my first day at school. I was their first child and they were nervous dropping me off. And they went round the corner and peered in through the window, and there I was helping the teacher hand out books and organise the class. Now, I don't know how true that is because I have no real memory of it, but I do know, even as a metaphor, that children find their rhythm.

Now along the way, I definitely lost it for sure, but if I look at the thread that runs through my timeline, teaching would be one of those great threads. But I have to say, I'm not all hearts and light and roses, sometimes I can be as cussy as the next person because everything to me sits in polarity. I believe there is a pole and a counter-pole. And to be aware of it gives choice of what to head towards or away from.

Sometimes we have to build new pathways for better choice, inside our minds to make a better decision-making machine.

Louie: Absolutely beautiful. And I've got to say, I you are

Chapter six: Louie B Free

wondrous. I was going to play *Shine On You Crazy Diamond* by Pink Floyd, but now I'm kind of debating Graham Bond's *Moving Towards the Light*. I'm not sure, but I'm just so grateful.

www.wfmj.com/louiefree

Chapter seven: John La Valle

JOHN LA VALLE

John La Valle is President of the society of NLP™ and co-author of the book *Persuasion Engineering*® with Dr Richard Bandler. I first met John in 2006 when I took my first NLP Master Practitioner and I've been learning from him ever since. One of my earliest conscious imprints from John was his phrase, "Tell it to me like I'm a 5-year-old, because when you can then you truly know it." That phrase has been a guiding star in my quest to become excellent in all I do. In this conversation recorded late summer 2020, we discuss how 3-D chess strategies work inside a business mind and look at the importance of growing new behaviours.

Chapter seven: John La Valle

Kay: So it's afternoon here in the UK and you're just waking up over there. We're all still in lockdown and I just wondered about that word 'lockdown'. It's a crazy word, isn't it?

John: Yeah, we're quarantined, but there's no law here telling people they must stay home. These are highly important suggestions and recommendations, but we can't be forced to stay home and not go out. And that's mostly because of our constitution, which I cherish every word of.

So, they use certain words here, and you and I both know a lot about words and their impact. So they wouldn't say 'lockdown', but they will say, for example, "We want you to shelter in place." Fortunately, most people understand what that means and that it's for their safety. I'm in New Jersey, and most people here are compliant. And stores can make things mandatory, so if you don't wear your mask, they don't let you in. So I understand you use the word 'lockdown' in the UK?

Kay: Yes, and I think it's just become one of those words that has slipped into common parlance. We use it without even thinking now. But knowing what we know about the impact of language on our words and pictures, if I slow it down and think about 'lockdown', it's quite a gruesome aggressive word. And yet somehow, it's become normalised.

John: Yeah, I don't like the word because of the impact I feel, the pictures I make. When I first heard lockdown, the first thing I thought was, "That's what they say in prison, when there's a riot, they go, 'we're on lockdown'." And I'm thinking, wow, if someone said 'we're on lockdown' here, I would think I'm in prison. I mean, I don't like the word itself, but like you said, the governments

Chapter seven: John La Valle

are slipping different words in and hoping they have different meanings. But this is what humans do.

Kay: The situation is fascinating, because it's giving us more of a chance to consider what we want to do and what we don't want to do. And actually, I really like this generalised ability to stay in one place, focused on one or two things of my choosing.

John: People have been asking what's different for us during this time. And I'm saying really not much, except that we're not travelling. My wife Kathleen and I are at home and online.

Kay: So John, one of the things you like to focus on is the precision of language, particularly in business. And the current business model has had to shift exponentially with many new ways of interacting with customers. Like most people, I now work largely from home; every day I'm interacting with the world on a small screen, with much less influence with my gestures and having to be more precise with my language. Does that make sense to you?

John: Yes, a lot actually. You know I like language. I think when I was younger, I had an intuitive sense about what was going on when someone would speak. I'd know what they meant and whether it wasn't going to go right or was going to go well. It was an intuitive thing, and I didn't know how to express that. I didn't know how to communicate myself in a way that was more precise so the other person would understand what I was wanting to say.

Language is very imprecise. You've heard the term, a picture's worth 1,000 words. I say, a word is worth 1,000 pictures. You just don't know which pictures a person has, so we take our best shot at it. But I find that, especially in business, people are ambiguous,

Chapter seven: John La Valle

yet they expect in their minds something that's more specific, and things don't go right as a result. So I'm guessing the opportunities for presenting our businesses in a different way, for example through Zoominars and webinars, are going to require a little upgrade in our skill set, so we can be even more precise. In the training room, we can see the responses from people, but behind the screen, we don't. When we're doing these Zoom things, there's a lot of information missing visually that would usually help us to understand what might be between the lines verbally, so that's a challenge.

> *"When I was younger, I had an intuitive sense about what was going on when someone would speak. I'd know what they meant and whether it wasn't going to go right or was going to go well"*

If I'm in a physical meeting with a group of people, I can watch around the room and see how different people respond to what the speaker is saying. On a Zoom call like this, with 10 people on it, I have to be watching 10 different screens, plus there's a lag in the transmission of the visuals. So that's another challenge.

I have a friend who's an expert witness, mostly for police officers in a situation where the officer is accused of shooting a person in the back. For example, the officer is facing a guy, and they see him draw a gun they think he's going to shoot, then the guy turns around and the officer takes a shot and ends up shooting the guy

Chapter seven: John La Valle

in the back. And that's a no, because the guy is running away. But there was a nano-second's delay in the communication going from the officer's eye to his brain. We're talking face to face. We're even talking online, you know, doing these Zoom calls. There's a certain delay in the processing of the data because our eyes don't see, our brain is what processes the images. There's such a lag between what they see – which is the guy is going to shoot them, and so the cop is going to shoot back – and in that very short space of time, the guy turns to run away. But by the time it registers in the officer's mind, they've already taken their shot, and they shoot him in the back.

That's just a comment on how much time it takes for us to register even the visuals. I don't even know about the auditories, but this officer does the visual thing in self-defence.

So in the Zoom call, if we're going to have a business meeting and I want to watch a group of people's responses, I've got to seriously upgrade my visual skills, my calibration skills, the whole thing. Because if I'm going to be in a meeting with people, I don't watch the speaker; I watch the people who are responding to the speaker. I'm looking around the table, I want to watch people's responses to what the person is saying, because that's really where the action is.

So that's just the visual aspect. The precision of language certainly helps in a situation like this. In a Zoom meeting, I see some people looking at their phone. They don't know I can see them looking at it. They don't notice, which is okay with me. I don't care what they're doing, but it means they're not paying attention to what's going on in the meeting.

A lot of people record Zoom calls, so we'd better be more precise with our language and it's still going to be misunderstood by, say, half the people.

Chapter seven: John La Valle

You know, a long time ago Kathleen and I were doing this seminar in Jersey, and there was a woman on the programme – a great, great lady. By the way, she'd been to a whole bunch of programmes – and I still don't know what she heard me say, except she tried to tell me what it was. But she changed her mind three times. In the middle of me explaining something to the class, she said, "John, I'm really surprised at you." I asked, "What? Why?" And she says, "I take offence to what you just said." I asked, "What did I just say?" I'm recording by the way, and she said, "You said X." I said, "Absolutely not. I wouldn't, that's not even in my repertoire." So she replies, "No, that's what you said." To which I replied, "Actually, that's what you heard, not what I said."

And then I said, "Okay class, how many of you heard me say what she said I said?" And half the class or more raised their hand. I was shocked, really shocked. And I went on with, "Okay, now we know what she said I said. Now here's what I say I said, and we're going to play the recording back." So we did, and I said, "So how many of you heard me say what she said, or what she heard me say?" And more than half the class raised their hands. I thought, "Oh boy. I hope when I play the recording back, I actually said what I think I said."

And I said, "How many of you heard me say what I said I said?" And of course, the rest of the class raised their hands.

And I told my audio guy to play it back through the speakers. And I said, "Okay, now how many of you heard me say what she said I said?" And only a couple of people raised their hand when they heard it this time.

This was a great lesson in listening and hearing. I said, "Now how many of you expected that someone would say, 'I have no idea what you said'?" I asked, "And how many of you heard me say what I said I said?" And the rest of the class put up their hands.

Chapter seven: John La Valle

And I looked at her and she said, "They're all wrong." And I replied, "I'm going to play it again."

I have to tell you, I must have played this thing back five or six times. I turned up the volume, I put headsets on her, we played it for her one more time. She was a great lady, by the way, she wasn't even arguing. She was like, "John, sorry, sorry." And she was pretty congruent about it. So I put headphones on her. I said, "Okay, I put headphones on you." And she said, "I'm really sorry, but that's what I hear you say."

And that was a good lesson for me. If someone says to me, "Well, that's not what you said," I reply, "You mean, that's not what you heard."

I was blown away by this. So now I have to wonder what goes on in Zoom meetings. I like the format, I like that we can do this, and then I think, "Oh my gosh, what can go wrong? What could be misunderstood?"

Kay: I'm discovering just that. What I experience is different to what I'm seeing in the playback, which is phenomenal because I have a new opportunity to smarten myself up because of Covid.

> *"Now I have to wonder what goes on in Zoom meetings. I like the format, I like that we can do this, and then I think, oh my gosh, what can go wrong? What could be misunderstood?"*

Chapter seven: John La Valle

John: On a Zoom call the other day, they were taking questions, and this was about persuasion, and a guy says, "So what can I do? What exactly, what specifically exactly, what specifically can I do tomorrow, actively tomorrow, what can I do to make a difference in my life?"

I'm thinking, "What do you want to know? Do you want a whole language session?" So I encapsulated it into one sentence, which was, "Well, first thing you should do is get off your ass and do something." And then I had to repeat it, but I said, "So what you really need to do is get off your butt," because I wasn't sure how that would be taken. Then I thought well, there's a portion of the audience that might think, "Oh this guy, he's so rude." That's what I meant when I said it because I knew it would have a different impact.

Kay: That's something you do so well – you're running an inside world and yet calibrating entirely in the outside world, but the free flow between the two appears seamless. And humour is that energy that seems to keep everything moving. And yet I know that you're calibrating so specifically. So tell it to me like I'm five – how is that for you?

John: When I was first doing NLP, I was working in a corporation. I had about 400 people in the same building, and the people who were my favourites were the ones on the bottom rung of the organisation who got the work done. And I loved working with them because they were the salt of the earth. And I find out the higher you go up in some companies, they get a little full of themselves. But when I was working with the regular people, I spoke regular language.

So we had to train them on something, and I was very specific.

Chapter seven: John La Valle

I'll give you an example – a company wanted us to rebuild their training manuals for running their machines, and we had no idea how to run their machines because we didn't work there. So we went in and did this project. We started out by saying we had to teach them basic stuff. I was trying to get across to them how important the specificity of the language was going to have to be in the manuals. And we told them, "If you guys are going to put this together, you could talk it into a recorder."

So we started out by asking them, "Okay, tell me what you do in the morning when you brush your teeth?" That's what I would do with a five-year-old, right? And when I do this in my mind, I'm thinking if I said to a two-year-old or a five-year-old, "Show me how you brush your teeth." I could figure it out from there but we weren't going to do all the work.

I have this crazy, innate ability to discover everything they could do wrong in my mind, then I start calibrating against that and then I correct it. Since I can figure out what they're going to do before they even get to do it, if I'm going to give them instructions, I already know what to change in the instructions. So, back to what I asked them, "So tell me, what do you do when you brush your teeth?"

They said, "I put toothpaste on a brush. I brush my teeth, like that."

I then started with, "Hold on a second, where'd you get the toothbrush from?"

They say, "Well, it's you know, it's in the medicine cabinet or it's in the glass."

I ask, "So how do you, when you say you take it, you get it, what do you get? How do you get the toothbrush?"

And they answer, "Well it's in my hand. I don't know."

So I ask, "How do you get it into your hand?"

Chapter seven: John La Valle

And they say, "Oh, I pick it up out of the glass."
I ask, "With which hand?"
And they say "Ah!"
Then we get to the toothpaste.

This goes on by the way, because I want them to understand that if they're going to teach somebody else how to run a machine by reading it in a manual, I want it to be as accurate as possible.

So then we get to the toothpaste, because I'm thinking a five-year-old is going to pick up the toothpaste, squirt half of it all over the sink, and a little bit is going to end up on the brush.

So I ask, "Then what?"
They say, "I think I put the toothpaste on the brush."
Me: "With which hand?"
Them: "Well, with the other hand."
Me: "And that's which hand?"
Them: "The right hand."
Me: "How do you put the toothpaste on?"
Them: "By squeezing it."
Me: "How hard do you squeeze it? You know, when you start squeezing, how do you know when to stop squeezing? So you get just the amount on the brush without squirting all over the place?"

Now this group of people, who are adults by the way, were blown away by this.

I go on with, "Listen, I'm not saying I don't squeeze a glob out of my toothpaste tube either, but I'm not exactly teaching you to brush your teeth right now. I mean, it's that simple. We're talking about you're going to put together how to run these machines and then we can get to the safety part of that, too."

Kay: So there's something about imagining what could go wrong, so you know, what's the next question?

Chapter seven: John La Valle

John: Well, pretty much. I mean, it's my way of being able to chunk down for them. I would say I'm practising what would happen in my mind. And if somebody asks, "Oh, what were their introductory eye accessing cues? And what was the first representational system? Or the first thing that came out of their mouth?" Listen, if you're not tracking everything you can track, then you'll probably miss something from the start.

Kay: Milton Erickson, who has obviously influenced a large part of NLP, talked about preparing himself so that the work was done ahead of time. And my understanding of that is that it was all about putting himself in the best possible state – a word that we use a lot in NLP – in order to be able to work with whatever came up. And there's something else in that which I see you doing. I know you're in a particular state where you're running those strategies, but it's seamless. So if I was to be childlike, I'd say well, I can concentrate or I can talk, but to concentrate and talk… And I know we do a lot of these altered states and time capabilities in NLP training, but just to upgrade a little bit more, do you have any more tips?

> *"When I'm training with people, I do whatever I can to keep the right chemistry"*

John: You mentioned a sense of humour, and when I'm training with people, I do like to make jokes or use humour. I do whatever I can naturally to keep all the right chemistry going. You know, the

Chapter seven: John La Valle

brain chemistry, as best I can anyway. When I'm going to get into a certain state, it's a very playful state.

You've probably heard me say that when I was younger, I played 3D chess. One came out with what I believe was a *Star Trek* set. There were three boards, three sets of pieces, and you played three games. Well, we didn't do that; we played three boards, three sets of pieces, one game. So you had three queens, three kings, six rooks, six bishops, etc. We had to make the rules up in advance. That was the creative part. So we had to negotiate: "What are the rules for this?" So we could say, for example, "You can move a bishop diagonally down from the top all the way to the bottom, if you want. But it couldn't be any more than X number of bishops on that board." So you had to create rules in advance because you weren't playing the game the way everybody else was playing.

Because I was okay at chess, playing it this way opened up a whole different way for me to predict what they were probably going to do. I'm not saying they would do it all the time. On a one-board game, I would say I can probably predict that 40% of the time. And with 3-D chess, I was able to predict it a little bit more than that, which I was surprised about. I think that's because I was able to calculate faster than the other person. Playing that game, I went into warrior mode in my mind.

It was like cat and mouse – "I'm going to play with you. I'm going to catch you." It was playful, and I think that's the sort of state I might use a lot of times when I'm doing training. And that also enables me because I'm watching the person and what they're doing. I wasn't so much calculating by looking at the board; I was watching the person, watching what they were doing. They could sit there and look at the board and start making the moves, but they would show them to me with their face, their posture shifts, etc. That was my calibrating.

Chapter seven: John La Valle

Kay: Oh, I struggle with 1D chess. I'm fascinated though, because when I play chess with someone who has an engineer's mind and is very good at logical, linear thinking, prediction and remembering rules, I notice they can remember all the combinations of what's possible on the board. Versus me, who's like, "Oh, I wonder what'll happen if I do this?" It's a left-right hemisphere difference. And I sometimes think good, because what you were saying about the chess board, if people are used to a set of rules and a one-dimensional chess board, then the moment you go into 3D, it takes them away from what's known for them, doesn't it?

John: That's exactly right. We all had to get Polaroid cameras, so that if we said we're done for the night, we took a picture of the boards. You didn't trust the other person not to start moving things around before we commenced later.

It was crazy because I started playing with prediction itself. I thought this was more about testing the other person because I wanted to know if they're trying to predict what I was going to do. So for a number of times, I'd be one guy who'd win 45 games in a row. Not because I was that great and he wasn't all that good, but because he'd watch my opening moves and I'm forgetting what they were, but a couple of opening moves and I chose one and I used it, I have to say, 10, maybe 15 times in a row, which should have given him a clue of what to do. But it didn't. So I'd make the opening move and I could see, and that's when I didn't even know NLP, but I could see him going inside his head and thinking, "I can't believe this guy is going to try this again, so I'm going to do something totally different." And he didn't have to do something totally different, but he did anyway. So that told me, back then anyway, "Could I predict how the other person is going to calculate how to predict me?"

Chapter seven: John La Valle

I remember back years with Richard, years and years when he was just coming back from the worst thing that ever happened to him, and we were doing Persuasion Engineering®. Before we start that seminar, usually he asks, "What's the seminar?" And I say, "It's Persuasion Engineering®." So I said to him, "You didn't ask me what seminar it was." He's ready to start. He's on stage. He's very congruent and he says, "Oh yeah, what seminar is this?" And I said, "It's Persuasion Engineering®." And he said, "Oh, okay." He said, "I got to tell you, John, I hope, I really do, that I remember what it's all about."

And I said, "Richard, I know you. When we open those doors, those people come in that room and you light up, you're just going to take off and you're probably going to do one of the best ones you've done. I'm not worried about it. If I was worried about it, you wouldn't be here on stage right now. And you and I'd be looking through the book and refreshing some things." He laughed at me, and sure enough, the people came in, they were all excited, so he got right into his state, and he went right on. And so, learning is state-dependent. I know you know that.

So that's the other thing. You know the other thing that's challenging about doing Zoom meetings with people? I can't even imagine business meetings. I don't know how many times I've asked someone, who says, "What am I going to do with my young one? You know, the blah, blah that I don't like to go to school?" My first answer to them is about changing the environment. Do something different, bring them someplace else, even for a week, and watch how they learn how to do something that's totally different. Change the environment because that changes their state.

They ask, "Where should I take Michael? Where would they like to go?" If they always wanted to go to the ballet, I'm going to take them to the ballet, but tell them they have to learn three things

Chapter seven: John La Valle

while they're there. It's the same thing in this environment here; you and I aren't in our regular environment. It's the same thing with businesses: half of them are sitting there in their jammies or whatever, so it's going to be difficult for them to get into that business-minded state. And you and I both know that's one of the most important things you can do – you've got to get to showtime. You've got to get into state, period, and then everything else is in there already. You don't have to be learning stuff, that's already in there.

Kay: I know that you teach that, and I teach that, and we know and believe it congruently. But even over the years of my NLP journey, it took me a while to really trust in myself – not in the technology of NLP, but to trust it in myself.

And so with these Zoom interviews, I'll have five minutes the day before framing the general thing and then I leave it because it's like, here we are, I'm in my state and trust the right things will follow. And I'm just doing what many of my colleagues are currently doing, which is running some online NLP trainings so that we've got people ready to move forward to Practitioner certification after the grand pause.

And again, I'm loving this because I'm only doing online workshops in two-hour bites and all I need to focus on is being in the right state. And then you know it's all there. There's something in my own personal journey about learning to trust that.

I want to go back to something you were talking about before, which is 3-D chess and the 3-D model, because I process my world in 3-D. Maybe other people do, I'm not sure. Certainly, the strategies I seem to have elicited so far don't necessarily match that. So if you were to share the 3-D experience of interacting with, I don't know, a small group of people, what's that like?

Chapter seven: John La Valle

John: I don't know, I typically don't know that I'm doing consciously. And again, that's the state that I use. It's not like I'm actually in my mind playing chess and they're all little pieces. That's not what I'm doing.

Kay: Yes, just to be clear, I didn't mean that we're talking about a game or a strategic play, but there's something more about the fact that I think a lot of people operate through life in a sort of digital, on-off way, but actually, when you expand it, there's more, if that makes sense?

> *'We're not in our regular environment. In businesses, half of them are sitting in their jammies, so it's difficult for them to get into that business-minded state"*

John: It depends on what they're doing. I wouldn't know everything they're doing unless they're describing it to me, even non-verbally showing it with their hands. I find that for the people who think in 3D it's more enriching for them.

I run into a lot of people who make flat-screen images of things, never mind movies or slides. I mean, it's a flat screen, there's no 3D to it. It's not like I describe it to people. There are a few other things I do besides being in that one particular state. I haven't even explained it to a lot of people. You asked, "Can you teach me everything you do?" I don't know that I can do that.

Chapter seven: John La Valle

You know, I'm a city mouse and my son, for example, he's a country mouse. So I can take a city mouse and turn them into a really kick-ass NLP trainer, because they've got the very best of situational awareness, and that means they can use that in the classroom. They can calibrate everything that's going on around them and they've got heightened senses of intuition.

But it's more difficult for me to take someone who's been a country mouse, let's say, and have to give them some kind of city mouse experiences. Or even someone who spent most of their life being a politician. If they're a lifetime politician person, that's all they've ever done, they've never had a job. They shouldn't be talking about business, and they shouldn't be talking about how to fix economies and all that stuff.

They should be talking about the best thing they know about, which is giving things away for free. That's my personal political opinion. Here in our Congress, we have business people, and they know more about what should be done. If I took a great guy or gal, a country mouse, and they went through college, university, the whole thing, I have more of a problem turning them into a kick-ass NLP Trainer than I would if I took a guy off the street, got him to quit the gang he's in, spruced him up a bit, got him a bit of an education. They'd probably be better at it because they have some of the basic skills that are really necessary in order to just calibrate people, the environment around them, and pay attention to what's going on.

Kay: That makes huge sense to me. My own experience, I'm a country mouse. I always lived in the country, but we moved a lot. So I was always the new girl in class. And you learn really quickly to calibrate. It's not just about the environment, city or country. It's actually your experience. And for a while it kind of went off track

Chapter seven: John La Valle

because hyper-vigilance can become a result of that. And certainly, it overwhelmed me for a while until I learned how to use it usefully, which is of course what we do with the Bandler® Technologies.

John: So I've got the country mouse, my son. He's about 14 at the time, and he wants to play in this band, rock and roll. They weren't rock and roll, by the way; I don't know what the hell they played. I know these guys and I thought they're probably messing around with drugs, so I told Kathleen, who's a city mouse by the way, and I said to her, "I'm going to go to New York, I'm going to take John Sebastian to New York." She said, "Oh, that's nice. What are you going to do?" "Well," I said, "I'm going to take him out to Washington Square."

And she said, "Oh, what for?" I said, "I'm going let him watch drug deals going down," because if you want to do drugs, that's where you went, you went to Washington Square Park. It's a big park in New York.

And so she said, "Are you crazy?" I said, "Yeah, well I know this is going to work because people need to have an experience to learn something."

See, we like to teach people in NLP, you give somebody an experience for something, they will remember it. I mean, it's got to be a good one. This is what my dad did to me, about drinking and driving. So I take John Sebastian there and there's all kinds of things going on, drug deals and whatever. And I said, "You sit over there," and I'm like about 15ft, 20ft away. "You sit over there. No-one's going to bother you because you're a kid." And I said, "You just watch how many people come up to me and talk to me, even just for a few seconds, okay? And I'm going to act like I'm already doing drugs and I don't really need any more."

So he watched and guys would come up to me and I'm saying to

Chapter seven: John La Valle

them, "Oh, man, I'm doing good. I'm doing good right now. And maybe come back tomorrow, see ya tomorrow."

So when I'd had enough of that, I went over to talk to John and said, "What do you think?" And he said exactly what I thought he would say, as any teenager would: "What, so you can come out here any time you want, buy drugs?" I said, "Yeah, of course, whatever kind you want, pretty much, but did you look around at all?"

He's a great calibrator, by the way; he always was. I said "Did you look around at all? We got a lot of guys, but you didn't look up in the windows in the buildings around here. You look up there. What do you see?" He said, "There's people with cameras." I said, "Yes, those are called police officers, probably DEA agents. What do you think they're doing up there? Having a cocktail party or something?"

He said, "No, they've probably taken pictures of everything that's going on down here."

I said, "Exactly, and now you and I are going to watch a drug deal going down." And I'm looking across the park – it's not that big – and I say, "Okay, you see the guy over there? He's got something in his hand. The other guy's talking to him now. They're swapping something between their hands. There goes the money. And there goes the drug. There it goes. A little packet. See that deal go down? So now we're going to follow one of them, you and me. We're going to follow one of them. Which one should we follow?"

He says, "We should follow the drug dealer." I say, "Why? The cops are going to get the drug dealer. We should follow the guy who just bought the drugs." He says, "Why?" I say, "So we can find out what he's going to do with it."

And we followed the guy, keeping enough distance away. He went into an alleyway, and I stopped to talk to my son. I said,

Chapter seven: John La Valle

"Listen, he's going in there. I'm going to give him a minute or two and then you and I are going to go say hi to him."

Sure enough, there we went. There's the guy in the alley, he's actually got the needle hanging out of his arm. And I looked at my son. I said, "What d'you think?" He said, "That doesn't look like a lot of fun." I said, "It's not a lot of fun. So think about this before you decide what you're going to do. Okay?"

Now to this day, he's not done drugs, and that's what I used to give my country mouse a city mouse experience.

My dad did it with me, by the way, with drinking and driving. He took me to a crash. An old early 60s Oldsmobile, which was like a tank. It hit a bridge. And I looked at it and I'm going, "God, so that's what happens when you drink and drive?" And I've never done it. I played in rock and roll bands in bars and clubs, nightclubs, and I didn't do it because I kept seeing the pictures of that old Oldsmobile. And that's something people don't realise. You've got to change the environment, even if it's for a short period of time, to teach something like that. That's a 3-D life experience, something that's live, not 'let me tell you what happened to me'.

"You've got to change the environment, even for a short period of time, to teach that…"

Kay: And it's interesting because a fair proportion of my work involves children and families and something I see an awful lot of is parents not allowing their kids to fall down and pick themselves back up. They try to save them on the way down or pick them

Chapter seven: John La Valle

back up, then go and shout at somebody and blame them. There's something important about actually feeling the experience neurologically.

John: And it's all senses. I mean to see, hear, feel, smell and taste. You know, there were smells out in Washington Square; it was the whole experience. And when we looked in that alley, it didn't smell good, and he couldn't wait to get out of there.

Kay: So going back to the business world that is now operating largely online where we have to be super-precise with our communication and we're only able to calibrate a little with two senses only, visual and auditory. If you were to offer strategies to enable people to start at least thinking about how they can smarten themselves up, what would they be?

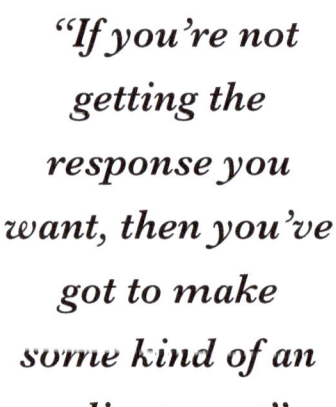

"If you're not getting the response you want, then you've got to make some kind of an adjustment"

John: You know, I still learn lots from Richard Bandler, just by listening and watching. Years ago, we were in San Francisco, and he said to one of his people, "Get me a Diet Coke and a glass of ice." And that's pretty simple, right? So an hour or two later, in comes in a big cart of desserts and drinks, sodas and juices and all this stuff. And Richard calls his assistant over and says, "What's that?"

She says, "Well, you said you wanted dessert and refreshments

Chapter seven: John La Valle

for everybody." He said, "No, get me a Diet Coke and a glass of ice."

And I sat there observing and listening to all this and thought, "Precise language." Precise, just precise, clear language. No beating around the bush.

So that whole thing is really about paying attention to two things: One is about what you say and how you say it, and that's not as important as the response you get back. If you're not getting the response that you want, then you've got to make some kind of an adjustment. Like if I say to a person, "What time did you start this morning?" and they say, "Well you know, what happened is, I had to go…" And I then ask, "Listen, what time did you start this morning?" It's all I need to know. I don't need to know what happened this morning. You went to get coffee… I don't want the story. I don't care about the story. I want to know what time you started because that's the only thing I'm concerned about right now. And that tells me they're thinking there's another answer I want, other than the answer to that simple question.

I like to watch Judge Judy, and one thing she does that I don't care for is the eye thing. She asks a person a question and they look up and she says, "Don't look up there, look at me when you answer the question." I want to send her an eye-accessing chart, and say "Judge Judy, you're great. I love you. I really do. You're fantastic, you're intuitive, you're smart, but you've got to stop this eye thing, because actually the person is trying to remember something." But what I like about her is that she notices them answering the question and what they do when they don't answer the question. That's what happens when people don't answer questions. They're wondering, "He's up to something," or "Why would he ask me that?" So in addition to me thinking about how I'm going to ask something, I'm thinking what's the response I get back? And is it

Chapter seven: John La Valle

even in the ballpark of the answer or the response I'm looking for?

I don't think people do that enough. And by the way, most people don't ask good questions in business. "What happened?" is a big question, like, "What happened yesterday?" Well, where do you want to start with what happened yesterday? I think in business we could teach people to be more precise.

I tell people that if I ask a question and the person goes off in another direction, I stop them and go back a little. Because for me, everything goes moment to moment. I don't need to listen to 15 minutes of blah, blah, blah. To me, it goes like this: you say something, I respond, you respond to that, I respond to that, you respond to that, I respond to that. And if there's a diversion, we handle it. Like, you brought me back once earlier today when you took me back to that 3D chess thing.

So, I like to work in short chunks when I'm working with somebody or teaching. I'm not going to get 18 sentences when there should have been a yes or no answer.

Kay: There are many things I've learned from you over the years, and one of them is the importance of well-targeted questions.

John: Years ago, one of my NLP trainers said he had something burned in and on his forehead. It was, "What is it you're trying to accomplish right now? Every time you start an interaction with someone else, what's your objective? Why are you even talking?"

And if I stay with that objective, I'll be able to stay more on track with other people. That's a basic skill. I remember in school being asked, "What were you trying to do?" I don't know how many times I've heard that, or "What did you do now?" You know, "How come you did that and not this?" I'd say, "Because I didn't know I could do this. That's why I did that." But in business we're

Chapter seven: John La Valle

all grown-ups. At least we're supposed to be. So we should at least have a better repertoire of responses.

Kay: I think that question of what's the purpose of the question is a vital one. And another one I often ask is, "Who is this about? What is the purpose of what I'm about to say? And who is this really about?"

John: In college I used to enjoy reading what's called the Uniform Commercial Code, which contains all the basic laws and statutes used by every country in the world. It explains all the little things, say the way your country deals with contracts and the way my country deals with contracts are basically the same. That's why I have another appreciation for precise language.

I love the fact that you guys in the UK have the Magna Carta, because that forms the basis of legal things internationally as well as our Constitution. Not because I like everything that's in it necessarily, but it's pretty straightforward.

If we use ambiguous language, then we get ambiguous responses. For example, there was a guy who got a parking ticket. He went to court, he brought his photographs, and the Judge said, "How do you plead?" He said, "I plead not guilty, your Honour." He said, "How's that?" He said, "Well, there's a sign there that says, 'No Stoping', and stoping means to dig holes." And there are no holes, no shovels, etc. The police officer said, "Your Honour, he knows what the sign means." And the judge looked at the pictures and he tore up the ticket. That's what rule of law is about. It's what it reads, not what someone thinks it means.

Kay: I've listened over the years to stuff from clients in various big companies who need this. I heard a CEO say, "How many times

Chapter seven: John La Valle

do I have to tell you?" And I think, "Okay, if it didn't land the first time or the second or the third time or the fourth time, who's responsible for that?"

I want to conclude by encouraging people to think about who they're hanging out with, because one of the great things for me about being with you guys in our international conferences, when we're all together supporting Richard's various seminars and yours and Kathleen's, is the exponential growth in our development. So who you're hanging out with, who you're interacting with, can be really powerful, can't it? And this has to be a time for new ideas, new opportunities, thinking out of the box and doing things very differently. It's got to be a time for harvesting what's useful from the past and moving it forward.

John: Yes, the landscape has changed, so watch where you're going, watch where you're walking. Things have changed out there. Companies are not going to be able to go back and do things the old way. The landscape changes because there's been a major shift for the whole planet. I think it's a good thing.

I didn't used to go shopping for my mother-in-law. Now I go shopping for her, and the first time Kathleen said to me, "My mom said there were some things she didn't get when you went shopping." My initial response was, "Oh man, I have enough trouble walking around a supermarket getting the stuff we got to get." I didn't say that, but that's the first thing I thought. And then once I did get all the stuff she wanted, I thought, "She's going to feel really good, she's going to have the stuff she wants, so what does she need this week?" So now I kind of like doing the shopping because I know it's keeping her happy.

Kay: I remember around 10 or 15 years ago, I was involved for a

Chapter seven: John La Valle

number of years with a national enterprise education programme. We would travel around the country running a sort of Dragons' Den, where we would take groups of college students and get them to come up with a business idea and pitch it to us, and we'd help them develop their marketing strategies. The activities were really about expanding their brains to think out of the box creatively, and the project was driven by research which showed what employers were looking for in their next generation of employees. They asked for skills like adaptability, flexibility, the ability to think entrepreneurially. And that resonated with me. I think those kids, who are now 30-something, are the ones who are going to move this whole thing on.

John: That's right. It's not the person with the most toys when they die who wins, it's the person who has adapted the best, most easily, and fastest to change. You've got to be adaptable.

www.purenlp.com

Chapter eight: Tracey Hutchinson

TRACEY HUTCHINSON

Tracey Hutchinson is a people development specialist and expert in the world of equine coaching, training, and facilitated learning. I work closely with Tracey in the development of Happy Brain, and she helped to establish our first Happy Brain Centre in a community riding stables which supports the mental and emotional wellbeing of staff and riders of all ages. I met Tracey almost a decade ago when she came to study NLP with me. Tracey is a valued colleague with whom I've recorded many coach chats online. In this mid-2020 conversation, we discuss overwhelm and other mind matters arising through our personal and professional lives.

Chapter eight: Tracey Hutchinson

Kay: I don't even know which week of lockdown we're in now. I've completely lost count and I'm feeling a little overwhelmed at the moment, there's so much happening. How are things for you?

Tracey: I think overwhelm has definitely been in my vocabulary a lot over the last few weeks, though I've made a concerted effort to weed out stuff I really don't need so that I can focus on things that I think are going to be of value. And that feels way better. I know it might get bigger again, but it feels way better than it did.

Kay: I think it's such an important process to go through. I've weeded out the non-essentials; I still need to prioritise, but my urgent and important lists are huge.

I feel that's something about this strangeness of time. You know, I took my watch off at the beginning of lockdown and I was determined to not be ruled by clock time. But right now I feel there just isn't enough time and I've got more to do now than ever before. It's all wonderful stuff, I'm really not complaining. The change includes having to make appointments to Zoom call family and friends, and I'm trying to keep up with lots of new WhatsApp groups. Does any of that sound like at all in your world or is it just me?

Tracey: Very definitely. Trying to find a new way of doing life with so many opportunities. I know you're really good at seeing something and going, "Well we could do this, we could offer that over there, we could bring that in. And what about this and look at those things and look at those shiny things over there, so we could do that as well." And then you obviously have your strategies for then going, "Okay, I've got all these shiny things, which ones am I going to really pay attention to?"

Chapter eight: Tracey Hutchinson

I think what people are probably finding is that their time has previously been structured for them because they've been at work or their children have been at school, and each day had a structure. And now we're finding the challenges of little or no (imposed) structure, whereas a bit of external intervention can be a nice thing because being allowed free rein to do it all for ourselves can sometimes feel like it's spiralling out of control a little bit. I don't know whether that resonates.

Kay: That reminds me, my dad uses a phrase; something about if you want to see a man's true character, give him everything.

And it's interesting because you know in psychology, they often put people under enormous stress to reveal their true selves; remove things from their lives, and things like that. But my dad always said, no, give them everything they want; with full freedom, they reveal their true selves.

> *"We have very little control over what's happening with the virus... but the more we can manage ourselves within that, the easier this time is going to be"*

And I think we see that in celebrity, don't we? We see that in people who can have absolutely anything and everything, and for some, the world then treats them like gods. That's where we see all sorts of unsavoury behaviours. I think Hollywood coach Michael Neill, in one of his coaching books or courses, has talked about

Chapter eight: Tracey Hutchinson

getting to know yourself when nobody's watching. What are your behaviours when there's nobody around? Again, that's a really nice insight. Sometimes when I have all the time I want, I can get quite lazy. My Dutch colleague Joost van der Leij, who has a model called Neurogram, tells me that my 'type' has a go-to relaxation place which is sloth! I wonder though if those are two exaggerated extremes – sloth or overwhelm?

Tracey: And if that sense of overwhelm is too much or too little, we're not in a place of balance. And that's quite often when clients make contact, where they have that overwhelm. They know they're not in a place of balance. And that happens – it's the nature of life, the ups and downs, the ins and outs, but having the resilience to be able to manage within those fluctuations.

And you talk about that in NLP and the Happy Brain model, being able to weather that storm with a greater tolerance level. I know I've had to review my strategy at times because I couldn't change the circumstances, but have learned how to manage with the circumstances. And I guess that's true for a lot of people right now. We have very little control over what the government tells us to do, what's happening with the virus, all those things. But the more we can manage ourselves within that, the easier the time is going to be. And the better off we'll be when eventually we come out the other end.

Kay: As we're speaking, I'm thinking about how overwhelm can arise as a single thought that drives intense feelings, or as unfocused attention to many thoughts. I'm challenging myself through the latter at the moment. They say we have 70,000 thoughts a day and 90% of them are the same ones that we had yesterday – repetitive auto-thoughts. Worries that can't be resolved by taking action can

Chapter eight: Tracey Hutchinson

become repetitive as the brain tries to figure a solution to each cycle of thought. That's a real thinking trap.

Tracey: I remember clearly doing an exercise years and years ago on a management training course; you'll know the one, where you've got a pie chart and you have to put everything in it that you do – I spend this many hours in 24 doing this, and this many hours doing that, etc. And I'd run out of pie chart way before I got to the end of all the things I had to do. It was a really simple way of visualising all that stuff, going through each part, as I know you will have done, and bargaining with myself, "Maybe could I do with two hours less sleep for now, maybe…"

It's interesting how we deal with what we're faced with. And lots of people right now are faced with, "How am I going to fill the next few hours before I go back to bed…" because there's so little in their day.

Kay: I see and hear that in people around me. And my stress response can sometimes be, "how is it possible to be bored?" And then of course, I step back and take another perspective on it – what might be true for those people? We all have our unique realities. I think there's something important here about planning; I think we need to be good at making good decisions and planning to be as busy as we want to be.

I wonder if people who find themselves in a state of inertia at the moment have previously been used to – and I'm looking for a pattern here – using stress as their motivator; filling time with urgent goals and deadlines. And when those are taken away, there's an absence of stress and an absence of motivation. It also reflects people's strategies for motivation that come from the inside or outside worlds.

Chapter eight: Tracey Hutchinson

Tracey: Understanding self and then finding strategies that work is both helpful and healthy. And being flexible too, because sometimes you have to do things in a particular way right now because that's what's necessary. For example, looking after a family member who's unwell. You may not get enough time to do yoga every day, which is what your optimum might be, but it's what's needed right now.

I think where we get a bit un-stuck is where we let unhealthy patterns become our way of doing things even when we know that it's not optimum for us, but somehow it just becomes habit and those new behaviours start to become entrenched. And again, I think that's quite a common point for clients to make contact, when they realise those habits and behaviours are unhelpful, and they want to find new ways of doing things that will take care of everything that they have to do and help take care of themselves as well.

> *"Sometimes you need an external input…It has to come from a place other than the place that creates the problem"*

Kay: It reminds me that all of us, even those of us in our professional field, sometimes need an external input; a perspective, a challenge, a question. But it has to come from a place other than the place that creates the problem.

Tracey: Absolutely. I think it's when people say, "Oh, you know, I don't want to go for coaching because it would mean I'm weak. I

Chapter eight: Tracey Hutchinson

should be able to do this on my own. I'll never live it down in my family…" I think that thinking of, "I should be able to do this for myself…" is great, and you know, most of us go through most of our lives being quite self-sufficient. And sometimes there comes a time when, whatever the circumstances are, having that external or just a different way of thinking about something can be the trigger that makes that difference, that 'Aha' moment which sets in motion a whole tumbling of things that help.

Kay: I think that's spot-on. Michael Neill, in one of his training sessions, talked about us as coaches; who's your coach, you know? Who's the coach's coach? And we're in the business of coaching, so we really need to be walking the talk. And I believe that it's so important to have good quality people around you, whether you hire them in or whether you just make sure that you've got somebody in your organisation, your team, your family, friendship group, whatever, who's going to ask that question, cajole you or re-direct your thinking. And I feel very blessed in the team that we work with that we can all help each other along the way.

I think it was Einstein who said, "You can't solve a problem on the same level of consciousness as the one that created it." Something I've heard a lot about over the last few weeks is the difficulty facing people living on their own right now, because as well as feeling lonely, they're missing out on those conversations that redirect thoughts or give a re-frame on something.

Tracey: I think then the challenge is finding appropriate ways of doing your natural thing. So before this, we'd often be using social media or watching the news or so on. And I love social media; when it works well, I could while away hours reading stuff that I didn't even know existed. However, I've also been at the end of

Chapter eight: Tracey Hutchinson

some of the disadvantages of social media, which has been a bit unfortunate. And when that's your benchmark, if you like, how distorted thinking can become, listening to the news and so on. I know we've both heard people talk recently about limiting how much media they're exposed to, and I do that quite deliberately as it is, because if I don't, I know how hard I have to work to come back to balance, having heard all that stuff. So yes, there are many challenges at the moment.

Kay: I just don't believe what I read or hear on social media; my first filter is that somebody somewhere is making a huge amount of profit out of this. The difficulty then is finding accurate information, so you have to go on a little investigation and look at potentially better-quality sources of reference material and science. So I view media generally as a source of entertainment, and that filter sets up my mind that I'm going to be entertained by this.

   At the moment, I indulge myself in one of the tabloids online, just to see the headlines, because I think it's really funny who's trying really hard to stay in the press at the moment. Of course, you've got the Covid headlines – what the government's saying, what the key characters are saying, what they should have said, somebody's opinion on that, what's happening elsewhere in the world, etc – then suddenly you see this celebrity who's doing something mundane, and somehow they've managed to get on the front page. Wow! How did they do that and why, and what would happen if they didn't? Those things super-amuse me; whose PR machine is working best and at what cost/benefit.

Tracey: It's an interesting metaphor; the stories we're told, and where's the nugget of truth. And I think quite often for ourselves, the stories that we tell ourselves about why we're doing things, how

Chapter eight: Tracey Hutchinson

we're doing things, and where the nuggets of truth are in that, that we might be better-served by listening to them rather than the stories being peddled.

Kay: That's such good wisdom. It reminds me of what we teach in our training, and I know right now we're about to dive into our online module on social narratives, personal narratives and family narratives, learning to discern and know what is useful.

Tracey: Yes, and what we have to let go of – that's important.

Kay: Speaking of our training, it's been so different delivering workshops and client sessions online hasn't it? Previously, when we met with our clients or students, we got to calibrate them and get a sense of all those subtle things, like how they move, how they walk, how they sit, how they respond in live time. And it's so different when you're sitting on a screen and you can only see a small part of someone.

Tracey: And you're seeing people in an odd set-up. Some of my clients have headphones on and I don't know yet how that changes the conversation, or the fact that the camera is located in one place, but I need to look you in the eyes, so I'm not really looking in the camera to look at you. And talking to my family as well; especially my elderly dad who is doing really well to get up to speed with the technology, but he's doing things like putting the phone to his ear when we're on video calls because he can't quite hear.

Kay: What I find so interesting is how rapidly we're changing as a society, as a planet. Yes, in response to a life-threatening virus, but also in smaller things that are really noticeable and measurable, so

Chapter eight: Tracey Hutchinson

that in six or 12 months, five years' time, we'll have adapted, and life will be easier.

Tracey: One of the things that I hope will come out of this is that we will make what we have to offer even easier for people to access. Some people will always want to see you in the flesh, but actually it's also very possible online. And I think that as we coaches get even more skilled in that, and our clients start to become more comfortable with it, even though we've kind of been forced into it, that actually it will make it more accessible for people who can't travel, are unable to leave the house for some reason, or are a long way away, and that has to be a good thing.

Kay: I'm already working with clients who previously refused to do Skype, etc, and now they just hop on. I recently wrote an article focusing on ways to thrive in this current situation. I wrote about endorphins, our body's natural opiates. They make us feel good, and right now we need something to help us feel good. Sometimes we must find new ways to laugh, for example because laughter is a wonderful way of boosting endorphins.

You told me recently about someone who'd unintentionally put a potato filter on their face during a work Zoom call, and you know that no matter how seriously you take yourself, you would have to laugh if suddenly the person on the screen looked like a potato. So one of my suggestions in my latest article is to do something crazy on the screen, like mismatch your clothes or whatever, because that forces the brain to do something different and go to new places; what we call in NLP a pattern interrupt. So we interrupt the pattern of, "This is how I normally behave. I'm normally very serious and I talk in this way, and I stay focused…" And we re-direct somebody's thinking into a new space, it's a wonderful thing.

Chapter eight: Tracey Hutchinson

I often feel there are two camps. There are the people who love laughter, who are always on the next strategy to find something funny in the world, and there are people who really hold on to being super serious and mutter that the other people are somehow childish. And they're the ones that I want to break through to and say, "Go on, do something silly; put your potato filter on."

Tracey: I'm reminded of a client I worked with recently. She was really – and I mean really – focused on her problem, she wasn't going to let go and she was closed to anything else because it was taking up all of her energy.

And sometimes that's okay, because you need to put your energy into something to shift it or do something different. But this particular conversation wasn't productive at all. So I did something that to some people might seem a little bit disrespectful, but I knew I had to do something to move it. So in the middle of this really intense conversation, I said, "So what's your cat having for tea tonight?" And exactly as you described, it just blew things apart and served really well to be able to move past and work much more productively. So now in my head, I have a potato – and that's

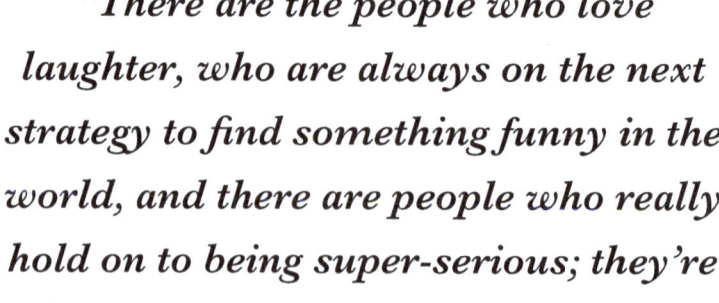

"There are the people who love laughter, who are always on the next strategy to find something funny in the world, and there are people who really hold on to being super-serious; they're the ones I want to break through to"

Chapter eight: Tracey Hutchinson

a shift for my thinking every time I need to, because we all get fixated on something and feel like you're going round and round and round the problem to no avail really, because it's comfortable or it just feels nice. We get a sense of 'poor me' out of it, or being justified in what we've thought or said or done. So sometimes you just need to chuck in a potato.

Kay: I love that; it's about helping people to help themselves, and sometimes it's not about doing the things that they want us to do; it's doing the things they need rather than those they want. Sometimes they need to find new places in their brains to go, and it can be life-changing.

Right now, I'm my office and I'm surrounded, as you know, by lots of gadgets and gizmos. And in a situation like the one you've just described, if I can't ask a question to break somebody's pattern of focus on their problems, I'll reach up and put on this pair of comic glasses and just wait. And they may go through an "arghhhhh" annoyed response, but ultimately, we have our responsibility to teach problem-focused brains to do something new, and then we can then take them somewhere else.

Tracey: That's right, and if I were focusing really intensely on something and you put those glasses on, I might be temporarily annoyed, but I would soon be into a great sense of relief.

Kay: And of course, we're not being trivial or flippant because in any coaching situation we've established rapport. We've made sure our clients trust us and we know what the margins are that we can take them to, because we've already calibrated that. So, just to be clear it's not a one-size-fits-all; we do what we do with integrity and with clear purpose.

Chapter eight: Tracey Hutchinson

Tracey: Yes, I was just going to say that clear intention is essential; it's about whatever's the smartest and quickest way to move through to solutions.

Kay: I'm remembering all sorts of funny times now. I remember a few years ago in a workshop, I was holding a toy magic wand while talking in metaphor about trapped giggles, and I gently prodded someone's lower leg using language that pre-supposed the trapped giggles would rise up into a laugh. Using language from NLP's Milton Model, like 'you know, it's just a matter of time', and 'I don't know how soon you're going to notice those certain sensations that let you know the giggles are rising', and 'the more you resist the faster the shift' and 'you know sooner or later they're going to come out…' And this particular person, who was a very highly skilled coach was like, "No, I'm not going to giggle. I'm not going to." But I set that language pattern up, "Well you know the more you try not to, the more it's just a matter of time…." And she did giggle and then laugh a lot, and of course it was a wonderful thing because then everyone laughed and got that lovely chemical bathe our brains and bodies need. Laughter is such an important way of being for us all.

Tracey: One of the beautiful things about being around children is that they're so unself-conscious a lot of the time. You know, even the things that they're trying to do seriously are quite often funny. And they're so quick to laugh at themselves as well.

Kay: Indeed, the purity of a child laughing! These times are certainly a challenge for our young people though. And I'm thinking a lot about teenagers who have made academic choices based on how the economic marketplace was. But now

Chapter eight: Tracey Hutchinson

that's changing rapidly, and future work trends are suddenly unpredictable. I wonder what type of jobs and careers will no longer be available to young people as a direct result of this situation.

And I've been thinking about the teenagers who haven't been allowed to meet up in groups, which has to be a recipe for disaster because biologically, teenagers are absolutely primed and programmed to be super-close, figuring out who belongs to which group and all of those things. On the other end of the spectrum are the primary school children who, with the best will in the world, could easily be labelled naughty if they go give a friend a hug.

Tracey: Yes, if they don't comply with the rules that seem to be being made up as we go along.

And I feel for parents because they're having to reassure their children while the children themselves will be picking up on how their parents are feeling, how the world around them is feeling, what's going on. I think it's quite a challenge for the whole family, not just the small person.

Kay: And we can't control the roadmap we've been given for what we can and can't do, like go to school, work in buildings. But we can control that space between our ears. And I feel very strongly that there are going to be some missed opportunities unless people listen up and start planning for themselves to be smarter through and beyond this.

Tracey: In addition to that, I think if you go out into the future and look back at this time, how do you want it to have been for you? What do you want to feel like about what you did and felt

Chapter eight: Tracey Hutchinson

like and so on, about how you managed this time? I think it's quite powerful for people to be able to say, "Well if I want to feel that about what I did right now, then that's what I need to do right now to enable me to feel that in the future."

We need to be encouraging people to start participating in that timeline, as well as going back to look for strengths they have from other times when they haven't felt that they've been in control. How did they manage to be resilient? What did they do? What can they learn that they can bring forward and start to do now?

Kay: I think the key word you used there was participation. Yet a lot of clients I work with have been living passively, as if they are a passenger in their own life. And actually, you know, when you start to get active and participating in your thriving self, it becomes a blank canvas upon which you can create a masterpiece that the future you will thank you for.

There's something in what you're saying that prompts me to think about legacy. I often ask that question, "What do you want to be remembered for? The person who went to pieces during lockdown 2020 or the person who just built themselves a stronger, better mindset and body and health?"

> *"There's something to be said for not making life complicated with those patterns we build up inside our heads"*

Tracey: And even if that's as simple as, "Actually, I kept it all

Chapter eight: Tracey Hutchinson

together and I kept my family fed and we kind of got by. We did the best that we could," that's enough. I think people are sometimes struggling with that concept that they should have built a new empire, that they should be making millions during this time, any of that stuff. Actually, just coming out whole is good enough, because that would have been hard work for a lot of people. I also feel sometimes that thinking gets in the way too much. When I watch my dogs and horses, there's something to be said for not making life complicated with those patterns we build up inside our heads.

Kay: Absolutely, there are so many dramas that immobilise people. I know we both take huge lessons from nature, and she doesn't care how hard we're trying. Trees and plants don't put in those extra thinking loops that slow us down.

We can make it much smoother and easier, take out the thoughts that get in the way and install a powerful thinking mind that's going to propel us in a useful way.

You know, each morning I open the curtains and look out, and I think to myself, nature is really happy at the moment. The sky is way bluer than I've ever seen it, the air quality is way clearer than I've ever experienced it, the birds sound more echo-y and multi-dimensional. Everything seems more vivid. The sensory experience is far greater because everything has gone into a state of pause. I know we're both lucky that we live in the countryside, but I believe it will be the same in the cities as well. There are lots of great things happening, things we need to pay attention to. And of course, by paying attention to it, you get a nice feel-good, so why wouldn't you do that?

Tracey: It's one of the things I encourage clients to do, paying

Chapter eight: Tracey Hutchinson

attention to all of those things. I know there's lots of stuff out there in terms of positive psychology, about gratitude, journaling and so on. Actually just bringing your attention to the positive, saying thank you for whatever it is that switches on those feel-good feelings. And then it builds from there. I think without fail, no matter how bad a day I've had, I can always find something that I can just go 'mmmm' about. It's in every moment, isn't it, really?

Kay: And it's smart brain training to bring your attention to those things because it's teaching your neural pathways to habituate them. So when times are bad, and our brains go to our most practised route of thinking, I often ask clients, "What's the very first thing you say to yourself when you get up in the morning, and what's the very last thing you say to yourself when you go to sleep at night?" I'm always blown away by people going, "Oh, I hadn't thought of that!" and then they realise how often they're setting their day up or trying to go to sleep with a negative thought direction that isn't going to work out so well for them.

I love the power questions like, "Oh, I wonder what fun I'll have today," or "I wonder what fun I'll have tomorrow." Or "what was the best thing about today" or "what could be the best thing about tomorrow…" Those simple opening and closing self-statements are really good for building brain juice that will ease the way to thrive living.

Tracey: I remember when I was little, and I don't know how it started but it became a bit of a sort of a family thing, every night before I went to sleep, I had to kneel beside the bed and say my prayers. It was as simple as, "God bless Mummy, God bless Daddy," and you had to include the dog and various goldfish, all of that. And I don't know why that was part of our tradition because

Chapter eight: Tracey Hutchinson

we weren't a particularly religious family, but what a fabulous tradition to have. Whether you're religious or not, just sending that out into the world and bringing your attention to those things that are special to human life is really simple, isn't it? So I don't kneel at the side of my bed anymore, but before I go to sleep I do cast my eyes around the family – furry family included – check in and go, "You had a good day?"

Kay: I think that's simultaneously complex and simple, because we're only beginning to scratch the surface of metaphysics and how intention can affect matter. You know, these things have influence over the airwaves and it does really good stuff inside, setting up those lovely oxytocin, dopamine, serotonin mixes. I think it helps if you can find a faith or a religion, or spirituality, nature, some higher-than-self acknowledgement.

We know that a lot of indigenous tribes direct a harmful spirit into the fire, and fire ceremony is a powerful shamanic technique that works with the intention to release something. And Guatemalan worry dolls help children secretly share their worries, believing that the dolls will absorb what they don't want to keep. I often ask children I'm working with to write their worries out on paper and then fold the paper into a tiny square before putting it in the bin or (an adult's) fire. There's something powerful in owning the release of emotion. It doesn't need to be shared to be healed. These are rituals that can bring comfort.

Tracey: You and I talked recently about values, individuals' values or society's values, and how we've seen a recent big shift in these. When we look closely at who's actually keeping the world turning right now… Obviously the people in the NHS, but also the people who empty our bins, the people serving in shops day after day,

Chapter eight: Tracey Hutchinson

the people caring for people who can't care for themselves. And traditionally those jobs are not highly paid, and they're perceived to be not highly skilled. There may even have been a perception that they were not really desirable jobs. But actually, these are the people who are keeping our country going right now. And even that shift away from what or who we thought was important has brought something else into focus. For me, that can only be a good thing; demonstrating the value of things that perhaps we've not really taken seriously before because we've maybe put our faith in things that were actually built on sand.

Kay: I agree, and I think it's such an important point. I guess that's where I was clumsily trying to get to with the idea about how the jobs world will change. But actually underpinning that is how we value certain jobs in society. I often have a little musing about if I was building an ark to survive Armageddon, who would I really want to have on it? What would be the really important skills to ensure safe passage? And it's an interesting philosophical exercise because it gets you thinking about who/what you really need – not want but need – to keep your own ark afloat. And we're seeing tremendous appreciation for amazing attitudes and skills now that we've previously not appreciated.

Tracey: Will you be outside clapping for carers again tonight?

Kay: Yes, I hadn't had it on my radar until last week when I got a text from a neighbour literally five minutes before it was due to happen, so I dashed outside. It was an emotional experience to hear the whole neighbourhood resonating with gratitude. And it got me thinking about those ancient practices of feng shui, where you clap to disperse negative energy. What a wonderful thing for the world right now. The second thing it got me thinking about was that the essence of gratitude each human was feeling, was really powerful for themselves and for the collective. To put that essence, that energy, out into the world can only be a good thing. You know, there are lots of studies that show that collective prayer practices in synchronised times have massively affected crime rates across the world. And we don't really understand how that works, but I think on many levels, this kind of thing is an important activity. So yes, I will be there, and I will be clapping.

Tracey: And of course, what we put out comes back, doesn't it? It's just another way the universe looks after us.

www.peopleexcellenceperformance.co.uk

Chapter nine: Kate Benson

KATE BENSON

Kate Benson is International Director of Education for the Society of NLP™ and co-author with Richard Bandler of the wonderful book *Teaching Excellence*. I first met Kate around 2007, when I took part in her Teaching Excellence programme. Shortly after that, I became a team member for her pioneering programmes in the world of NLP in Education. Through Kate, I met our colleague Julie Olsson and we three share deep passion and commitment to helping the next generation flourish. In this conversation, recorded mid-2020, Kate and I discuss our respective experiences of supporting children and struggling families through lockdown, building resilience for the times to come.

Chapter nine: Kate Benson

Kay: Today I want to talk about the next generation, which is something that we're both heavily invested in. So Kate, we're in lockdown; what's on your radar from parents, teachers and children?

Kate: Well, we live in interesting times. I've been spending a lot of time talking to teachers and parents, and my acronym for the moment is SOS. It's about Strategies, it's about Opportunities, and it's about focusing on Successes.

I think children are giving us a very interesting message. When I ask them what they don't like about lockdown – a term I dislike by the way, and I'm encouraging people to find another word that works for them because 'lockdown' feels so restricted – most of them say, "Oh, I miss my friends." And when I ask them what's good about this time, virtually every one of them says spending time with their parents.

That's a big message to put out to parents; to say okay, you might be worried about how much learning they're doing, how much English or maths or science. You might be worried about how much structure they've got in their day or whether they're online too much. But actually, what they're enjoying is your time, and it's lovely that they have that now.

This is echoed by parents. Initially there was a shock of course; the, "Oh my goodness, how do we do this? I've got to spend 24 hours, seven days a week with my children." Which, let's face it, most of us haven't done since they were babies. But once they managed to relax into it and let the rhythm develop, I think parents are starting to relish this because they realise it's time-limited. So the O in SOS is about relishing opportunities, the time that you've got now to do something different.

Many parents are too conscientious about home-schooling.

Chapter nine: Kate Benson

They're the ones thinking, "Oh, we can't possibly get through this; how do those other people do it?" Well, they don't. Teachers aren't worried about the parents who are worried; they're worried about the children who aren't resourced. We're in the same storm, but we're not all in the same boat, and there are a lot of children who are in a not very good boat. Take those who aren't getting vouchers for their lunches. Some schools have to prioritise getting packed lunches out to kids because for those children, it's more important than lessons online.

There are others who haven't got access to the internet, iPads or computers, and they will be stuck in front of the TV because that's what's available to them. My concern is for those children. Most teachers aren't going to worry about whether or not your child has kept up; they're going to worry about the ones who've been left behind.

Kay: That echoes very much the conversations I'm having with parents, teachers and children. Children are telling us they love and appreciate this time with their parents. And there's something fundamental that we seem to have lost sight of or ignored, which is that kids are learning every second of every day. The question is, what are they learning? If they're learning to get attention from their parents in unhelpful ways, then they're going to do that anyway. So I get what you're saying about this opportunity to tune into what your children need from you, which is nothing to do with the national curriculum.

Kate: Absolutely. I've been doing webinars recently with parents, and the big question I like to leave people with is, "What do you want your children to learn from this experience?"

People who've read my book will know that one of the things

Chapter nine: Kate Benson

I say all the time is that the children won't necessarily remember what they've learned, but they'll remember how they felt about it. They'll remember their feelings at this time much more powerfully than whether they learned to do quadratic equations.

So my question to parents, and to teachers to some extent, is what do you want your children to take away from this?

I'd like them to take away a sense of being compassionate and kind. You know, the lovely things, the things they're learning from what's going on around them.

People are doing things differently. We've got women sewing scrubs, people delivering and making food, all sorts of lovely things. People say we're in this together and let's do something to help others. Those are the things that I think children can learn from.

Kay: It's capacity-building really, isn't it? It's building an infrastructure for a more connected future of community and collaboration; a different way of working together, rather than what I saw a lot before this, which was parents complaining that their children wanted to be in their little own space with their screens and disconnected from the family. Now there's this opportunity to reconnect to family and to community.

Kate: That's true, and I think the question you have to ask is, why were they doing that in the first place? A lot of parents say that now they're spending even more time on screen, but screen time in itself is not necessarily a bad thing. It's a neutral thing, neither good nor bad; it's what you do in it that's important. Teenagers have always spent lots of time in their rooms. We did; it's just a thing that happens when your brain and body is changing. It's where you want to be, making your connections with your friends.

Now they do it through their phones. Way back, it was everyone

Chapter nine: Kate Benson

listening to the Top 20 on the radio on a Sunday afternoon. There's always something teenagers do that connects them. And the few moments when your teenager turns their attention away from their screen and looks towards the adults in the house, what are the parents doing? Well, they're on a screen, so the moment is lost, and the kid goes back to their own screen.

Now, because parents are paying attention to children more, children are paying more attention to them. I don't claim that all teenagers are going to have joyful relationships with their parents, because they're not; that's not the nature of being a teenager. There are all sorts of lovely things happening, though. People are eating together again, cooking and baking together, because parents aren't running them to ballet class, football coaching or extra maths tuition, whatever. Sitting down to a meal is special time; these are ways of building connection.

Kay: So when our children tell their children about the grand pause, or whatever we choose to call this period in the future, they'll remember how they felt. And when we make parents and teachers aware of that, they have a chance to help children to feel differently about their situation.

We know that always starts with the self. If I'm working with a family, a classroom, a team, etc, I find one stable person to become a beacon for the rest. And that puts the responsibility back onto the adult to create the feelings you want the children to adopt for the future. Is there a technique you'd like to share to help somebody to become aware that, while that's a great responsibility, actually it's easy to do?

Kate: I think the first thing is to be aware of the question. To have that as your point of reference when something's happening.

Chapter nine: Kate Benson

For instance, little Mary is throwing Coco Pops at little Jonny. So you can breathe and say to yourself, "What do I want them to take from this situation? What do we as a family want to take from or learn from this situation?" This raises your mind out of the minutiae of the detail of the Coco Pops into what we call in NLP a meta-position, where I can say, "Okay, what is happening here? What do I want to take away from this?"

> *"We will get through this. It will pass. It will be a relatively short period of time. So let it go. it doesn't matter if there's milk on the floor or Coco Pops on the table"*

Often, the trigger for an argument isn't the cause. It's a good idea to ask the question, "What do you think we're actually arguing about here? Are we actually arguing about the toast? What's behind this?"

I think in a more positive way, you can think, "What is it that I want us to take away from this? How can I make sure they learn something lovely from it?" And breathe, take a moment for yourself to move to a bigger picture before you respond, and relax.

Richard Bandler was talking about this the other day; we will get through this. It will pass. It will be a relatively short period of time. So let it go. It doesn't matter if there's milk on the floor or Coco Pops on the table? It will pass.

We're coming up to the 75th anniversary of VE Day – the end of World War 2 in Europe. My parents' generation were teenagers,

Chapter nine: Kate Benson

some of my uncles were younger, the same age as the kids we're talking about now, and it's interesting to hear what they took away from that situation, which went on for six years. I'm not talking about people who were fighting, I'm talking about people who were at home, when awful things were happening around them. My parents were in Hull, which was the most bombed city in the UK outside London. They were bombed-out, but they didn't talk about that, they talked about going to collect eggs from their grandparents, playing out, and the rosebay willow herb growing on the bomb sites.

Whatever we do, children are for the most part quite resilient. We can do a lot, as you do Kay, to build more resilience, but actually, they are quite resilient, and they will make a good situation for themselves. And I'm heartened by that.

Kay: Yes, there's something in what you're saying which is about NLP timeline. You know, so long as you've got your eye on the big picture, you know where you're heading.

I used to do that with my kids. If I got into an argument with one of them, I'd think, "How do I want my relationship to be with them in future?" And that would take me straight out of that intense moment in time and keep me orientated in a future direction.

Kate: Absolutely, and as we know, the brain goes where it's sent, and that's a really important thing to remember. That whatever you're focusing your attention on, whatever you're thinking about, is where your energy and your physiology, your thoughts and actions, will all line up. So make sure that every thought is the most useful one you can and let everything else back you up on that. Because as you said, that's exactly what happens.

Chapter nine: Kate Benson

Kay: And it shifts energy and flow, smoothing and moving inside our brains and behaviourally. As you were saying earlier, often you can see somebody's shoulders relaxing when they suddenly realise it's much easier than they were thinking.

Kate: I think so. I want to reassure these parents that everything will be okay; that we just need to wait this out.

Because we're all a bit isolated, there's a lot of fantasising going on. So, the school stuff – I refuse to call it home-schooling, by the way, because we're not home-schooling, we're trying to make school at home. There's a difference; home schooling is a choice that people make, while this is just getting through, having some school stuff going on at home. I see people fantasising about what other people are thinking about them, parents fantasising that the teachers have an expectation that they will do all the stuff the teachers are sending home, and the parents will be graded by the teachers.

I saw a lovely post on Facebook from a school inspector who had graded himself as the School at Home. His gradings included 'Absolutely Dreadful' and 'Awful'. So there he is, saying, "I can't do this either. I've got a 12-year-old who doesn't listen to me and a 14-year-old who won't come out of his room."

On the other hand, I was talking to a group of teachers from a fee-paying school. There was a huge amount of pressure on them because the parents have high expectations, and they're trying to record wonderful lessons at home. They don't have specialist equipment, just their phones or computers, and when they make a mistake, they think they have to start all over again. Their fantasy was that the parents were sitting watching these classes and judging the teacher's performance.

So I said to this group, "When you're in class, do you ever make

Chapter nine: Kate Benson

a mistake?" And they said yes. I asked, "What do you do?" And they replied, "Oh, we just put it right." So then I asked what the difference is between doing that in class and when you're recording or teaching a lesson online. I said to them, "You're not making a major movie production here. You're not expected to be producing something of Hollywood standard."

Kay: I get that. And there's something in there about dividing our attention. You and I would both teach people to give their undivided attention, to hold the space for the learner or learners; and in doing that, our bandwidth has to be completely expansive. But if you take up half a chunk of your own bandwidth with, "What do the parents think of me?" then you've already limited the outcome for the people in front of you.

Kate: Yes, and the minute you have that thought on the inside, where's your attention? If you want to do a really good job, you want to put all your attention on the outside, on the people you're communicating with. The minute you go inside, you'll fall over your words, stumble, worry or whatever. It's also about where you are. You can be inside or outside your own self, but not both.

Kay: It's back to flow. I want to pick up on something you said about the fear of being judged. I find that fascinating, because one thing that's come out of this situation for me is that suddenly I'm spending time looking at myself on the screen and thinking, "Oh, do I really look like that?" And I'm listening back to my recordings and saying, "Oh, that's not what it sounded like in the moment."

And I can use that information to become better, more focused, more determined and whatever else I need to do. But I know colleagues who are crumpled by what they see and hear, because it

Chapter nine: Kate Benson

hasn't matched their internal picture. And I wonder if that's part of what some teachers are experiencing; they're being faced with feedback that doesn't match the picture and sound.

Kate: That's right. We're not good at feedback or feed-forward. We're not good at constructive feedback, we're not good at processing unhelpful feedback and being able to choose what we're going to pay attention to. And I notice talking to teachers, that those who are really doing a great job with their students have all of those loops running. One of the things I say to teachers and parents is that nobody knows what they're doing!

Kay: That's true [laughs].

Kate: None of us know what we're doing, nobody's been here before, so we have no idea. So the best way to approach that is in a spirit of experimentation. I see teachers who three or four weeks ago had no clue because they'd never delivered classes online, and now they're experimenting and doing amazing stuff.

Some people will be familiar with the idea of flipping your

"If you want to do a really good job, you want to put all your attention on the outside, on the people you're communicating with. The minute you go inside, you'll fall over your words, you'll stumble"

Chapter nine: Kate Benson

classroom, which means slightly different things to different people. Essentially, it's handing things back to your students, your learners, to do the questing, and I'm seeing some really exciting stuff going on. I know a teacher, a Teaching Excellence graduate, who's getting his students to write the course books for next year's students from their point of view. He's asking things like, "Hey, how would you rate this, and what would you like to have had when you first arrived on this course?" So they're being creative in trying different things.

Take the fitness instructor Joe Wicks, who's online doing a half hour PE class in his living room every morning. It's so simple, and practically every kid in the country is doing it, plus their parents and grandparents.

When a teacher sends work out, it wallops some parents because it takes them back into their experience of school. For some, their feelings about learning that subject aren't good, and they have to try to overcome that to help their child with the task.

It's a road to nowhere, and teachers aren't yet recognising that. I've had messages from people saying, "Oh, I feel so terrible. I can't do this, it's horrible!" And I've said, "Well don't. Don't do it." Or I ask if they know somebody who loves that subject. One parent I know face-timed their uncle in Ayrshire to help their nine-year-old with their maths and the uncle really enjoyed the contact.

If you enjoy baking, maybe you could run a baking session with a group of kids on Zoom and give two or three other parents or carers 45 minutes to themselves, and then they can do the same for you? How easy does it start to get when we collaborate like that?

I don't like the word 'lockdown', and I don't like the idea of 'socially isolated'. We're not 'socially isolated', we are physically distancing, not socially distancing. We can socially be closer.

Chapter nine: Kate Benson

Kay: I agree, it reminds me of when my children were small. Every summer holiday, a group of us young mums would take it in turns to lead an activity. It might be baking or planting something in the garden or making a model.

Kate: That's right. The other thing that comes up in a lot of my conversations is that some parents are feeling guilty because they're not 100% enthusiastic about spending 100% of the time with their kids. And they feel guilty that they don't want to be an enthusiastic playmate, teacher, parent.

What are they feeling guilty about it? It's not always that exciting, you know? If you have a baby, you can only go "goo-goo-goo-goo-goo-goo" at them for so long before it gets tedious. And who wants to spend all day playing with an eight-year-old, apart from an eight-year-old?

Of course you don't want to do those things all the time; you want friends of your own age! I worry about parents who say, "Oh, you know, my daughter is my best friend." Well, get a friend of your own age, because why would you want an eight-year-old as your best friend? You're a parent, you're not best friends.

Anybody who's had a toddler and plays tea parties for hours, pouring and drinking tea, knows it's mind-numbing. That's why I think sharing these things out between us so people get a break is good. I've said to parents, let them sit in front of the computer or watch *Frozen* for the nth time. Take an hour out. Have that time for yourself. Build your resilience. Build what you need, and then the next hour you can be present for your child to play tea parties, teach maths or whatever you're doing that hour with enthusiasm, knowing that later you can have some more time to yourself. And I think that moving in and out and not expecting to be there 24/7 is important. You have to build space within your space.

Chapter nine: Kate Benson

Kay: That's sound advice. As you're talking, I'm thinking about the parents who discover something about themselves during play. Let's not beat ourselves up!

Kate: That's right. And you know it will pass. The worry and the fretting does more harm than just letting it go.

Parents are saying, "Oh my, how many hours should the kids spend online?" And this isn't the time to have that conversation. Whatever works for your child is what's important.

We have some children who thrive on massive amounts of structure, so give it to them. There are others who baulk against that and want to use this time for more freedom, so let them do that.

The other message that's important for parents is that you and I have known many children and we can make helpful suggestions, but it's important that parents remember they are the expert in their child. Making choices that are right for them is important, so let's not generalise. Things will be different for each child, even within the same family.

I worked with one family where the parents lived their work. The father said to me, "We work hard, and we play hard." But I noticed that what they were playing at was very structured. They went on mountaineering holidays and so on; their trips had an outcome.

The first child slotted perfectly within this, so they were happy doing that. Then the next child came along, an entirely different person, and it was hard for the parents to understand because they had this perceived wisdom within the family that that's how they did things. You have to be able to be flexible with your different children, and value the different things they want to do. One of them might be very structured and another one might not be. Go with the flow.

Chapter nine: Kate Benson

Kay: Absolutely. And those are really good messages. You use the SOS acronym – Strategies, Opportunities and Success. If we jump into opportunities, what I've seen up until now is a lot of silo teaching. You know – now we're going to do history, now we're going to do maths, now we're going to do English. And at the moment, that seems to be where a lot of parents are struggling, because that's not their usual life. You and I are in the business of building life skills, and I've been admiring a family near me recently. The children are outside virtually all day. They go in for a couple of hours of proper teaching or whatever it is they're doing, but otherwise, they're outside. I was watching them bouncing on their trampoline and thinking about the cross-curricular opportunities in that. Like count and bounce maths, bouncing in rhythm to poetry, making body shapes out of vowel sounds, turning in the air towards the past, the future, the east or west. You could run a whole cross-curricular lesson just with trampoline bouncing.

> *"It's important for parents to remember that they are the expert in their child"*

Kate: Absolutely! I'm a school governor and I work in schools still, usually training to find a whole-school approach to something. Quite often, there will be what they call suspended-curriculum weeks, or theme weeks, where the normal timetable is suspended and there's a theme. It could be VE Day or landing on the moon. One of my students said to me, "The curriculum is the Trojan Horse, and when we pick up a theme, whatever it is, it gives us the opportunity and it gives children the opportunity to deep dive into them."

So you take a theme, and there's always the maths, the language skills, the written skills, the research skills, the science, the geography, the history, within anything you choose. It's so much better. Even though I spent years, like you did, as a teacher, teaching to 45-minute slots, I still don't understand why we have these rules.

Parents aren't skilled teachers, so teachers are helpfully sending a timetable home because they want to help the parents. But what are you interested in as a parent? People are baking, they're growing things, they're learning about finance. Take our friend Julie Olsson. She's a geography teacher and I once said to her that it must be wonderful to know all about the different landscapes when you're out. She said, "Oh no, you see what I really love is soil." I've never thought of soil as being interesting, and Julie enthused me about it. There's biology and chemistry, measuring, all sorts of things, in any subject you take.

"Take the little girl at the funfair learning about velocity, centrifugal force and maximum speed just by going on the rides with her dad, with deep excitement and joy glued to the science"

I think this is a really good opportunity to deep dive into learning

Chapter nine: Kate Benson

something and allowing you skills to coalesce around whatever the topic of interest is. As you said, something as simple as bouncing on a trampoline.

I tell a story in *Teaching Excellence* about a little girl being taken to a funfair and learning all about velocity, centrifugal force and maximum speed just by going on the rides with her dad. And deep, maximum excitement and joy and pleasure is glued to all the science. How fantastic is that?

Kay: And as a society we seem to have lost sight of that. At the moment, I hear parents say, "Oh gosh, I have to teach my child." And that seems so ridiculous when I think about what I've learned recently. In the last six weeks I've learned how to create an online training programme, I've learned how to navigate Zoom, I've learned how to communicate in a different way on social media. And the reason I've learned is because I've wanted to. So if we ask parents, or any adult, how do you learn? What are the conditions for your learning? Then you can kind of take away that need to 'teach' a child.

Kate: Yes, and I think that's just because of a lack of information. One parent actually asked me how to get their child to see them as an authority figure. It's the idea that you have to put a different hat on – a parent hat, a playmate hat, a teacher hat – and you can't be all of those things. It takes me back to the lovely phrase you use – let's not be a sage from the stage, let's be a guide from the side. And that's all a parent can expect to be. Unless you want to go and retrain to become a teacher, then sure, go and learn a set of skills if you want to. But it's not necessary and you don't have to.

I also encourage people to think about what a teacher is. A parent is always the primary teacher for a child. You teach them

Chapter nine: Kate Benson

how to learn all the most important things before they go to school. They learn to walk and talk and feed themselves; all of those things are your responsibility, you've taught all of that. So you do know how to teach your child. It's about keeping on doing what you've always done and not suddenly trying to morph yourself into another person.

Kay: Yes, we do these things for the child, but I think sometimes we get confused and make it about us. Am I a good enough parent? Am I a good enough teacher?

Kate: That's right, and I'm sure there'll be plenty of competition in some parenting quarters about who's doing it best. It's the same with the SATs [Standardised Assessment Tests] children here in the UK have to do aged 6-7 and 10-11. Those tests were set up to measure school and teacher performance, yet very quickly they've become the basis for school gate conversations about which child has done best.

I wouldn't even be giving SATs results out because it's not about competition. Some parents will compete – who's the best parent, the best teacher. And that's not a great position. There's only one thing worse than being a completely neglectful parent, and that's being perfect.

Kay: [laughs] That's right!

Kate: I know adults who are still trying to get to be as good as their parents because they hold a view of how spectacularly fantastic their mother and father are. But it's better to just be a little bit imperfect. Take Bruno Bettelheim's book, *The Good Enough Parent*, and be guided by that, because good enough is good

Chapter nine: Kate Benson

enough. Having some flaws is a good thing, because how else does a child learn to accept their own mistakes, flaws and idiosyncrasies if they're measuring themselves against something they perceive as perfection?

I think there will be a lot of people out there trying to compete, which is why they're trying to stick to the timetables. Going back to where we started with what's on my radar right now, what I would like parents to take away from this experience is to stop being helicopter parents, stop being competitive as parents, stop thinking they have to be everything for their child and give them all of everything to be the best. Because actually it's not helpful. I was thinking about what my mother would have been doing if we'd been eight or nine during Covid-19. And you know, she would have probably still said, "Off you go; come back in a couple of hours for something to eat if you need to. I'm having coffee online."

Our parents didn't have an expectation that they were going to provide every moment of attention and entertainment and resource for their children. There was an understanding that children doing stuff on their own for themselves was a good thing. And some of the time maybe that pendulum was too far that way, but I do think in some cases it has swung too far the other way. I'd like to see a little bit more equilibrium, more balance between giving children our time, our resources, our attention, and allowing them to learn by just allowing them to be. We don't need to watch them on the trampoline in the garden; they're quite able to do it themselves.

Kay: That takes me back to my childhood and the hours we spent freely roaming our doorstep forest or how we made dens and rose petal perfume factories in the garden. My father's enduring

Chapter nine: Kate Benson

message was that we all needed to be able to grow into adults who could successfully navigate life.

I wonder about the S for Success as I think back to having my first child in the 1980s. My go-to childcare bible was Penelope Leach's *Baby & Child From Birth to Age Five*. One of the questions she posed was, "How will you know if you've been a successful parent?" Her answer was, "If you like your children when they're adults." And while I don't necessarily think that's the right answer – if there is a right answer – it's a good question to ask. And it brings us back full circle to the beginning of the conversation, which is that we need to be looking ahead a little bit, don't we?

Kate: Absolutely, and with a giggle and forgiveness for ourselves because nobody knows what they're doing right now. We don't know what the outcome of this situation will be, and people find this not knowing hard to live with. People are fearful about that uncertainty, and we need to find a place where we can accept that not knowing.

It was actually like that before, but we pretended we knew what was going to happen. We booked a holiday in June and that meant we were going to go on holiday in June. The chances are we were, but actually something might have happened to prevent that, so none of us have ever really known what tomorrow will bring. But living with the current uncertainty is very hard for some people. I think it's a good thing because it means we live more in the moment. We're more present in our own lives and for our children's lives, rather than being somewhere else. So I think there's much to be said for accepting a certain degree of uncertainty. It's interesting to look at the media. As soon as there's a hint about some development, the media is saying, "Okay we're in lockdown, but when are we coming out, how are we coming out, how is it

Chapter nine: Kate Benson

all going to happen?" The media is constantly trying to get the answer, and that's a reflection of us.

Kay: There's a whole other conversation in there about how our brains seek familiarity, the illusion of control, the ability to predict the future. But as you rightly point out, it was all an illusion anyway, wasn't it?

So, thank you Kate, for your SOS acronym: Strategies, Opportunities, Success. Strategies for thriving, Opportunities for new ways to aim our brains towards Success.

www.meta-nlp.co.uk

Chapter ten: Chris Cummins

CHRIS CUMMINS

Chris Cummins is a pal, colleague, and inspirational business leader who I've known for several years. He is the author of the book *Power Presenter*. Chris and I spend hours exploring, planning, and delivering initiatives for wellbeing and human development. This interview was recorded in early March 2020, when we were in the US as part of the international training team supporting the seminars of Dr Richard Bandler and John La Valle. We had no idea of what was ahead of us and just a couple of weeks later we both scrambled flights back to the UK as the world suddenly locked down. In this conversation, Chris reveals his commitment to the wellbeing of his staff, colleagues, and customers.

Chapter ten: Chris Cummins

Kay: Chris, we've just had the pleasure of a few weeks' immersion in the latest Bandler® Technologies here in Orlando. We've both been involved in the NLP for many years, so tell me your NLP journey.

Chris: Well, I've been involved with NLP for around 13 years, and the whole journey has been amazing. I'm a Society of NLP™ Master Trainer and I have great fun being around the team on trainings like this. I learn so much from Richard, John, Kathleen and all our colleagues on the International Training Team.

Kay: Yes, we meet several times a year as part of that crew, and I really appreciate what you said about how much we learn together. Each time, we learn from and inspire each other, as well as being inspired from the top. Chris, I know you use NLP in your everyday life and in business. You're a Master Trainer of NLP in Business and you run a global company called OTD.

Chris: Yes, OTD stands for Our Training Department, and a lot of the work we do is corporate training; anything from skills training to coaching, both one-to-one coaching and in large groups. It's a really good organisation, and one of the key things is that all of us use NLP in some way in the content and delivery of the programmes. So what we're doing is really trying not to just tell people they need to change, but give them ideas on how to achieve that.

Kay: That's interesting, as we both work in the field of bringing out the best in the people who work for us and with us, our clients, customers and so on. It reminds me of a conversation you and I had recently around mental health and emotional wellbeing in the

Chapter ten: Chris Cummins

workplace. This is a really big issue for us at the moment and there are a lot of initiatives, certainly in the UK where we both live, based around supporting mental health and emotional wellbeing in the workplace. But often I find these things are really just paid lip service. You know…"Come and talk about your problems," but there aren't the supporting skills that teach people how to think on purpose, behave with good intention with appropriate outputs, and feel good for no reason. What do you do specifically to support the wellbeing of your workforce?

Chris: We've actually got a Wellbeing Tsar within our team, and in our team meetings we have a wellbeing item as part of the agenda. As a business, what we've really focused on is bringing the best out of each team member. For us that includes things like flexible working, because we believe people work well at different times or are most productive at different times of the day. Some people work better in the mornings, some people work better later in the day, so we give people the scope and flexibility to be able to do that.

Our Wellbeing Tsar Sue goes out to research things that will help to bring the best out of each person within our business, and she brings those to the table at our team meetings. For example, we might do some kind of meditation or some positive anchoring to help people boost their confidence or be in a nice, calm state when they're answering the phone. All those kinds of things happy, and we take this seriously and have fun at the same the time.

Kay: There's a lot there about state management, which is a term we use a lot in NLP. And when we can help people to discover for themselves how easy it is to re-balance, re-set their emotional state, it puts them back in the driving seat, doesn't it?

Chris: It does, and when you think about that in terms of standing up in front of an audience, one of the reasons I run NLP Business Practitioner and Master Practitioner programmes within our business is in order to make sure we're giving our customers the best possible experience.

So for us, state management is everything. So a lot of the time I will focus all our team on making sure that they really make the customers feel great.

Kay: And that starts with feeling great yourself.

Chris: Absolutely.

Kay: It's interesting. You talk about supporting flexible behaviour in your workforce by encouraging them to take responsibility for what their needs, wants and work patterns are, and that requires quite a lot of insight, doesn't it? It requires personal insight to not just play a system of, "Oh I'm not a morning person therefore I can't go to that meeting," versus "I know I'm optimised at a certain time of the day."

How do you encourage, or how does your tsar encourage, people to learn more about themselves in order to take responsibility for the way they think, behave and feel?

> *"We've focused on bringing the best out of each team member, which includes things like flexible working because people work well at different times of the day"*

Chapter ten: Chris Cummins

Chris: Well, we've dedicated a lot of resource over the last two years. We had a company come in and focus each individual on what makes them work best in the workplace, and as a result of that we analysed all the data.

My business partner and I worked in the pharmaceutical industry for decades, and the way we worked there was very rigid. So we thought, well, is that still applicable in the modern workforce? Does it work well? The answer was no, and the data was there to support that. So, we had a big conversation with the whole team. We started talking about flexible working and what that could mean. We also put some limits in there because the customer is the most important person, so if there's no-one there to answer the phones then we've gone the other way. We've managed to do it and get it to work, and yes, it does take some discipline. Our office manager makes sure we have cover, and that the team are working well together and within themselves.

Kay: I love the terms work well and working well. As you know, in my business we have a service area called Work Well, which is precisely for that. And you help organisations support their staff to work well in a holistic way – emotionally, physically, mentally and socially as well as economically and so on.

I know you and I agree that our staff or our customers bring to the table whatever's going on for them in their private lives. For some people, coming to work is their only bit of sanity, and for others it's where everything kicks off. So, if we just for a moment think about what goes on in people's home lives and maybe in their communities, I know you're involved in supporting community youth work, and we know how important it is to have that support before people even get into the workplace, so we want to encourage them to look after themselves.

Chapter ten: Chris Cummins

Chris: We do, and interestingly my business partner and I look after each other; we try to make sure we're both okay. There are things we do to keep ourselves healthy, like exercise, trying to eat the right foods and getting a good night's sleep. Those are the kinds of things we really focus on as the bare minimum, and bearing in mind that most of the people who work in our business are significantly younger than us, we do our best to encourage them to do the same. At the same time, there's a social aspect to our work as well. So one Tuesday a month the whole team will go out to a pub quiz, because we know that bond is important; good teams work well together and normally play well together as well.

I've got to tell you what happened today. I was on a Zoom call with a lot of people. We've just launched a new initiative, and the only contribution I made to that conversation was to ask one of the people, the biggest big project manager in that session, how they were. We'd gone into task mode, and I just stopped and said, "Just stop a moment. How are you feeling?" The biggest smile came on the guy's face, and we went on from there. I think that generally we don't do that enough in the workplace, because we get so focused on the task. Part of what we have to do as a business is notice when people are feeling a bit under pressure and actually say, "Are you okay? Is there anything we can do to help you?" Because, like you said, sometimes people are bringing stuff from home into work.

Kay: That's true, and in my client work I see a lot of adults who are struggling in the workplace and in their personal lives, and they are totally linked. Some people feel isolated and lonely. They don't have somebody to listen to them, they don't understand how to let go of the problems of the day, so they bring them home. It interferes with sleep, they drink or eat the wrong things, and it becomes a negative spiral. So actually, you leading as a role model

Chapter ten: Chris Cummins

is a great example, because you're encouraging your staff to do something very similar.

Chris: The other things we avoid are those classics like sending emails after work and at the weekends. Those things can add to people's stress because they feel like they've got to read that email when they're with their family, for example. I'm not saying our workplace is all rainbows and unicorns by any stretch of the imagination, but we do make a conscious effort to make things a lot better in the workplace.

Kay: So we've talked a little bit about the adult world, what people bring into the workplace, the things they're dealing with in their home lives, and the skills we use with NLP to encourage people to think smarter, feel better, behave on purpose with integrity, and so on. As you know, one of my great passions is the prevention model. We see so many adults needing mental and emotional support or intervention, as I see it, and in a smarter world we would prevent the need by teaching children better thinking skills. Chris, you've been a great supporter of my book *Happy Brain*, which is very strongly a model of prevention with many strategies created from what children tell us they need.

Children in a play environment quickly reveal how they're already beginning to stack up what we call in NLP deletions, distortions and

"I'm not saying it's all rainbows and unicorns, but we do make a conscious effort to make things better"

generalisations in their language. You know the sort of thing, "She looked at me that way, and that means she hates me, which means everybody hates me, which means I'm going to have to move school…" Those thinking traps cause havoc in the small mind and in social groups. So we're encouraging all parents or those working with children to be able to gently coach children out of those patterns, to help them to see a different way of responding.

In Happy Brain training, we have a very simple exercise called undoing thinking traps, where the children learn five challenges to their language. We ask – What else could it mean? What's the worst? What's the best? What's most likely? What would somebody else think it means? These are really simple steps, and a very powerful introduction to NLP. You have children, yes?

Chris: Yes, I have four children with my wife, and one adult child with my ex-wife.

Kay: So five children, and I have five children. And when my children were young like yours, I didn't have this skill set; I didn't understand what I know now. Of course, you have an amazing skill set now, while your children are small. Are you consciously aware of how you use your NLP skills, for example, to encourage your children to have better operating systems, for want of a better expression?

Chris: Yes, and just to re-frame all of that, you know as a parent that you can get emotionally involved in lots of things, so you need to be able to disassociate yourself from the situation with your child before then, before doing any kind of intervention and hoping that it's an unconscious thing that you're doing anyway.

I love the five patterns you were just talking about because some

Chapter ten: Chris Cummins

children are experts at distortion in their minds. I've got a 12-year-old daughter, a 10-year-old daughter and twin boys aged eight. And when I watch them sitting at the dinner table having a chat, it's a great time to really work out what's going on. Or at least it's a snapshot in time when they're all sociable children. It's hilarious; my wife and I sit there and think, "Wow, where did that come from?" And you have to resist the temptation to step in and solve things for them straightaway. The pacing and leading side of things is really important.

With one of my boys, I think a lot of times I can challenge some of his distortions just by texting. I guess the key thing is that it allows me to have a dialogue with him that I didn't have before, and we're both disassociated from it, so we can have really good conversations that way. And you know, an eight-year-old child typing stuff compared to a 28-year-old is completely different; you get good clean communication, which is really good.

Kay: I've heard other parents say that. But it's a double-edged sword because one of the biggest complaints I hear from parents is that their children spend too much time on screens, whatever the situation may be.

However, as you say, it does give the opportunity to get somebody to see the language that's coming out and be cleaner about the way it's used.

Chris: From my perspective, sometimes I'm away from home for long periods of time and it gives me and him the opportunity to connect when we couldn't have otherwise. So I like it. I feel much more connected at home now because they've got these devices.

Kay: Because when you're away, you've maintained contact?

Chapter ten: Chris Cummins

Chris: Absolutely. It's great, and what's really good is that my son set up the app in order to be able to communicate with me.

Kay: Moving on to something else Chris, you and I value being of contribution to our respective communities, so we both volunteer in different ways. I volunteer with a number of charities, including as a Samaritan, and support people who are really struggling with their mental and emotional health. You also have a very strong view about contribution to society. Could you tell us something about that?

Chris: Well, on my journey from the train station to the office, there are many homeless people. My business partner noticed it as well, and all our team members. And we thought, we've got to do something about this, so how can we bring the Work Well thought process and philosophy into some kind of community work? So we started looking for charities we could volunteer for, like the homeless charity Shelter. And we thought we would all have a go at volunteering and seeing what it's like to work in one of these places for a day. And it's been brilliant.

 We say, "Well guys, you don't have to do it if you don't want to," but everybody feels they can add something, and we're going to continue doing this work. For us, that's just giving back. The people within our business want to do it, and they want a way of being able to do it.

Kay: It's so inspirational, because on the one hand, you're this role model for your organisation because you look after your health and wellbeing, and your business partner does the same. And you're being of community service. Do you think the tide is turning? We're of a similar age and I think there's been a disconnect from

Chapter ten: Chris Cummins

other members of society; I think some people have become very boundaried and territorial. But there seems to be a tide turning, an awareness of how we can connect with others beyond our immediate social group and support the needs of others as best we can.

You've chosen homeless people as an example of how you can reach out and change some people's lives and influence your staff at the same time. Do you see that chunking back into the global international business model that you have? If you think about your business plan, is social contribution a significant part of your business?

Chris: Yes, in business parlance it's one of our critical success factors. To the point now where we create resources for our trainings on sustainable materials; that's come from feedback from some of our planet-conscious customers and from the team.

Kay: Do you think other larger organisations have a true social conscience, or do they apply a broad brushstroke? I hear a lot of lip service being paid to social conscience.

"I think some people have become very boundaried and territorial. But there seems to be a tide turning, an awareness of how we can connect with others beyond our immediate social group"

Chapter ten: Chris Cummins

Chris: Well yes, but in their defence, some organisations appoint somebody to do this and it's only a part of their job, so it's not even in their objectives. You know, they've got to do all their work and they have to do this as well, and when it comes to appraisal time, that goes out of the window. I think that's where it falls down, and where it could end up being lip service.

Not all the customers we work with are 100% focused on it, but there's one company we work with which has made it part of their CSF [critical success factors]. I did some strategic planning with them last year and they take it to the point that their company cars are all electric. So they've really gone to town with this, and the way we can help companies do that is by citing examples from others.

Kay: Yes, good practice looking for good practice. So that's good practice in the environmental sphere, and that's something you're aware of within your own organisation and you're noticing good practice in other organisations.

Finally, I'd like to draw us back to what we term mental health. It's such a buzz word for us in the UK at the moment, and I think it's not a very helpful term since it's a health we all have. But we know what it means. So it's easy to say yes, "I'm driving an electric car, I'm recycling, but I'm going to take antidepressants because I can't cope with the world and I'm going to close down internally." For me, I see that there isn't enough fluidity in the big picture of wellbeing.

Chris: I don't know how many of my customers are in that situation, but I can say that we have a lot of NLP-trained people and their job is to help people to change their state, so they're changing their internal brain juice. Our role is to create the

Chapter ten: Chris Cummins

environment for people to feel great with every interaction they have with us, and mean it, so fully congruent, not just flicking on a switch and doing it and then going back to our own grumpy selves. You know, it's all about actually living that life.

Kay: Which brings me back to Happy Brain, where we major on just six neurochemicals out of more than 100, but I chose six that we can easily influence. Like when you were talking about social gatherings that connect people in the pub as a great way to increase the hug hormone oxytocin, or boost serotonin by taking some time out, and probably your favourite Chris, releasing endorphins through laughter. So it's really profound isn't it, when you see this chemical interaction that's spreading through the workplace?

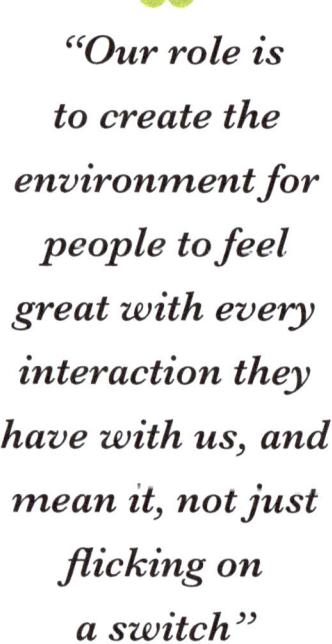

"Our role is to create the environment for people to feel great with every interaction they have with us, and mean it, not just flicking on a switch"

Chris: It's great. I love those aspects from your book, because all these years I've been telling team members, why don't you just mix a cocktail of states up; it's all in there.

Kay: Yes, we talk a lot about state but I'm never sure everyone really understands the chemical flux surging through our bodies and how that process is so easily influenced by, as you say, things

Chapter ten: Chris Cummins

like sleep and active movement, contact, connection and just having fun.

And we're both about to take part in another Neuro Hypnotic Repatterning® [NHR®] course with Richard Bandler and John La Valle. We've both assisted on it many times and we love it so much. It's such a treat to be a student and take downtime from our busy lives and invest in something special for us.

Chris: Absolutely. You know, it's always good to just keep that energy going. And you never stop learning.

www.otd.uk.com

HEIKO WENIG

Heiko Wenig lives in Germany where he is a renowned teacher of energy, consciousness, and healing. I've known Heiko for many years and he is one of my most favourite examples of a human truly flourishing. I'm continually inspired by his mindset and abilities, and I love that we share so many perspectives around growth and learning. As I was bringing this book together, it felt a little odd that I hadn't recorded a conversation with one of the people I speak to most often, and who connects with so many in this book. Thankfully, he agreed and here we have our conversation recorded in February 2022, which begins with a discussion about the word thriving.

Chapter eleven: Heiko Wenig

Heiko: I didn't know the word thriving, I had to look it up. Is it a common word in English?

Kay: I think so. It's certainly a word I use a lot as a direction for people. I'm always wondering how I can orient people towards their thrive state. But it's also a word I interchange with flourishing. Do you know the word flourishing?

Heiko: Yes of course.

Kay: So thriving, flourishing, and another word that comes to my mind is vibrancy. And for me, that's a bundle of words that sit together. And the ancient Greeks used a term called eudemonia. I love that too.

Heiko: Well, it's interesting because I wouldn't use the word thriving. I love the word flourishing though. To me, it has energy and power. But I hardly use the word thrive because my picture of it is pretty misty and it only gives me the direction, I suppose because many things thrive and it's a very neutral thing. So fungus can thrive also as roses and cherry trees.

Kay: That's so interesting, how one word can make such a big difference in our minds. So what do you think about the word chaos?

Heiko: My picture of chaos in connection to these times is like a house falling down because of an earthquake; a complete mess, like a natural catastrophe causing chaos. But for me, the thing we're talking about isn't a chaos. When I think about the sub-title of your book, *Thriving Through Chaos*, I wouldn't call the past two

Chapter eleven: Heiko Wenig

years chaos; I see it as challenges. But chaos is of course one filter people have used during these times and that's why they feel like they're stumbling.

If you get into chaos, it puts your belief and value systems to a test, into a proving state. Then you get the opportunity to either set new directions and re-orient yourself, or put more strength in the orientation and direction in which you're already travelling.

Kay: When I swap the word chaos for challenges and say 'thriving through challenges', that brings a picture into my mind of the resilience tools for dealing with challenges. Whereas if I say chaos, then that implies a lot more instability.

Heiko: I think this time has definitely been chaos for many people, especially those who have relied on solid, fixed structures for stability.

Kay: By fixed structures, you mean their beliefs and values?

Heiko: Yes, because rigid beliefs and values don't offer much flexibility, whereas the more you can constantly aim towards flow – being in the flow and flowing with it all – then it's not chaos, it's just a challenge. Many people have been inflexible, relying on fixed structures for stability.

Kay: I love that. You've re-framed the meaning of the word chaos for me, as I can see the difference between being *in* chaos and looking *through* the challenges.

The next word that pops up for me here is resilience. We seem to hear and use it almost daily. It's such a throwaway term; people say they want resilience, and that's a nominalisation because it isn't a

Chapter eleven: Heiko Wenig

thing at all – it's a process of doing. I think it's a shallow word.

Heiko: To me, it's a fashion word. The resilience movement popped up a few years ago and became a fashion, so now everybody, even in politics, is now talking about resilience, yet I wonder how many people really know what it means.

For me, resilience is just the starting point. I'm unhappy that so many people focus on resilience because the word includes a bit of a fight against something; it presupposes that there is something to be resilient against or with.

And that may be true for some things, but it's like looking at the problem rather than beyond to a picture where there is flexibility and dealing with things in a fluid way. Of course, I know resilience is what people talk about, but for me it is too focused on the problem, going through a hard time.

Kay: And the opposing forces within that hard time…

Heiko: To me, it could feed fear because there's a potential threat for which you need resilience, so it could be dangerous, maybe

"...chaos puts your belief and value systems to a test. Then you get the opportunity to either set new directions and re-orient yourself, or put more strength in the orientation in which you're already travelling"

Chapter eleven: Heiko Wenig

even health-damaging in terms of burnout because there's always a bit of friction. But that's my very personal opinion.

I've got the same opinion about 'protection'; you know, in the energy world where everybody is saying, "I need protection here, protection there…" and I think yes, that's a starting point and sometimes it's really useful and necessary to consciously protect yourself, but I have a completely different aim, which is to be in the state of energy where you don't need any protection because you're not resonating with the threatening or dark or evil things. And the best protection, so to speak, is love and freedom.

Kay: That reminds me of many conversations I've had with people about these things, which just seem to set up more barriers in the world.

Heiko: Yes, and a basic picture of the world of fear. Although of course, it's sometimes necessary and useful to protect actively and consciously, to be energy-wise protected. To me, it's like hand-washing. You know it's necessary and useful, but I'm not spending my whole day looking at my hands and imagining how dirty they might be, constantly hand-washing, hand-washing…

Kay: Talking about hand-washing, you and I both have very old dogs we often talk about. And I've been thinking a lot about people's relationships to their pets during lockdown times and how that may have changed when people went back out to work.

Heiko: I've got different opinions about that. On one hand, I think people were very glad that they already had pets, but we had a fashion during lockdown where pets were sold out and puppy prices went up three, sometimes four times the regular price.

Chapter eleven: Heiko Wenig

Many pet homes were nearly empty, but now I think it's turning around again, the pet homes are getting full again and the pets are no longer wanted. To me, that reflects my point of view that Covid brought to the surface people's inner structures of decisions and directions.

Kay: Would that happen in any challenging situation, or was this different?

Heiko: Of course, every intense and demanding thing that happens in life will bring out inner structures, but Covid by itself was completely different, and also energy-wise, so it also worked differently.

Kay: How was Covid different energy-wise?

Heiko: Oh completely, on every level, because it was a global thing you had to face whether you wanted to or not. Everybody was confronted with it and couldn't work around it. There wasn't a single corner of the world where you could say, "Okay, I'll go there and I'm safe." Even the South Pole Station had Covid.

So the deeper inner structures – beliefs and values – helped direct people, as they thought, "How do I deal with that?" Everyone was confronted with fear in one way or the other; inner fear about business, work, money, home, relationships, family, everything. So it hit every level, which is incomparable to other things that have happened in the past, because even the world wars hit most of the world, but not all of it.

Kay: So I'm thinking in metaphor that the whole world has been shaken up, literally?

Chapter eleven: Heiko Wenig

Heiko: Absolutely, and that shaking brought up the deepest structures. Of course, from a spiritual point of view it was very interesting; the compassion part and also the motivational part in terms of vaccinations and why people got their vaccinations.

Kay: Do you think these times have allowed people to become more conscious of these deeper structures within themselves?

Heiko: Absolutely. It was a great opportunity, the greatest opportunity, because everybody was forced to look at that which they couldn't get away from. It was everywhere; the first time I know of where everyone in the world had to face something similar in the same conditions, one way or the other.

And it brought up the collective structures, you know? It was so interesting to see how different countries reacted to the same thing. So I think it was the greatest opportunity.

> *"Many people went into their creativity to find new ways of thriving they had never thought of"*

When I thought about recording this interview today about thriving through chaos, as you named it, I thought the chaos, so to speak, was pretty much the same everywhere, and people everywhere faced the unknown in different ways. Including medical-wise and political-wise, again and again. And also right now, we still have to face the unknown.

Nobody could say, "Okay, it's definitely going to happen like this…" because no-one knew. At the beginning, you didn't know if a vaccination was possible, then you had it and thought it would last forever, and then no, you have to get another one. And recently with the Omicron variant, it could be endemic, or maybe not; nobody really knows 100%. To me, that was very interesting, how people were reacting.

Kay: But we never really knew what was ahead of us anyway, and that for me is all part of the wake-up to the illusion of control that people perceived they had in their worlds. People would say, "I'm definitely doing x in June and going to y in July…" And while there was of course a high probability of accuracy before the pandemic, we couldn't truly predict our futures. I find it fascinating when people say, "I can't plan anything. I can't predict anything because it's all so unknown…" because we only ever planned and predicted based on a calculated illusion that we knew what was coming.

Heiko: Absolutely, and Covid brought that to the surface. The illusion of control was a big thing – everybody was faced with it, had to look at it and deal with it. And that was very interesting work-wise, how some businesses had to close down or had terrible problems because of the rules and laws passed. And then we saw how many people went into their creativity to find new ways of thriving they had never thought of before, for example quickly becoming expert at setting up a small television studio at home. But others just got stuck, and broke.

From a neutral point of view, I was interested in how people dealt with the challenges coming to light, and energy-wise, the whole thing was so unique. Discriminating structures of society didn't apply anymore; it wasn't about poor and rich, it wasn't about skin colour, it wasn't about religion, and it wasn't about political systems. Everyone on every level in every structure had to face the same. And that's completely unique.

Chapter eleven: Heiko Wenig

Kay: It's been a great leveller, hasn't it?

Heiko: Yes, even the richest people in the world got Covid, and the poorest ones. Of course, there were differences in medication and access to support, but all sorts of people died from it – the very rich with the best medical care, and the people in hospitals which had no oxygen tanks.

Kay: When you were talking a moment ago, I was thinking how people in a battle can stay fixated on the mud in front of them, or look beyond the mud to see where they're heading and find a reason to keep going. The orientation of perspectives is how people get through, get beyond, and head towards the bigger, brighter future. Conversely, they can imagine everything collapsing in on them.

I saw a big contrast in that way between the collapsing into helplessness and those who, as you said, used their creativity to think, "Come on, what have we got to do now? What are we going to do differently? How can we orientate ourselves towards the new future?" Did you see it that way?

Heiko: Yes, and on the other levels as well because the motivation was also so different. So a lot of people are getting through this because they made the decision to make the best of it, while others got through it with fear. But they still got through it. Others didn't though.

And one of the challenges, to follow your metaphor, was to look at the mud on front of you and the bright future at the same time, while constantly walking through uncertainty.

From my perspective, darkness is mostly, if not in all ways, fear-based. And when I looked at it from that perspective I saw fears

Chapter eleven: Heiko Wenig

on every level – personally, family-wise, society-wise, economically. And it brought up fear as a basic reaction, so it became a frightening situation. Some people became aggressive and angry, even cruel. Numbers increased for cruelty at home, in relationships, child abuse, riots, demonstrations and so on.

On the other hand, there was a big wave of compassion and looking out for each other, taking care of neighbours and those in need. And all from that split, which previously existed but is now showing up more precisely, some people just looked at the mud. For me, one of the challenges was, and somehow still is, to look at the mud in front of you and the bright future, or the future, at the same time or constantly, back and forth.

Another challenge energy-wise was to look at the brightness and the possibilities in the mud in front of you, knowing you can't change it. To me, one of the basic decisions everyone had to make, and still must make, is the decision, light or dark?

> *"The orientation of perspectives is how people get through, get beyond, and head towards the bigger, brighter future"*

Kay: So when people make decisions, sometimes they make them because they have a high degree of certainty and clarity from their inner self, from an internal strong, grounded, aligned perspective. But some people need a little support and help in making their decisions, and they look around and take some guidance or

Chapter eleven: Heiko Wenig

influence from the outside world. And I saw many people looked for role models on YouTube, in books or podcasts, to find out how successful people were coping to get some guidance and inspiration from them. Others simply defaulted to the general media. Do you know what I mean about people seeking guidance from inside or outside, and if so, I wonder if you could talk a bit about that?

Heiko: What came to my mind immediately there is yes, but that's already after the first decision about in which direction. Fundamentally, it's looking for the positive or the dark side. And you're right, people are looking for guidance. Nobody knows everything about everything and it's absolutely natural to get guidance in fields of life where you're not an expert. But the decision light or dark was already there, and the role models people are listening to are often decided by an algorithm; so you get what you seek. And that created bubbles of consciousness that enforced everyone's opinions of, "I'm right." And the information they found reinforced their opinion, so it got more solid in both ways.

But it also brought up a contrast of getting more into the positive or more into fear. There were ridiculous demands made of politicians, stupid questions from journalists who are attacking when they say, "Tell me how it will be in three months…" because no-one knows how the thing will be in three months. But they still wanted promises because they were desperately looking for something to hold on to, seeking a structure from the outside just to feel more secure in the moment.

So many structures were revealed – of personal insecurity, fears, motivation, decision-making, acting, reacting and interacting with humans in every possible way.

Kay: I'm also wondering about the counter-example to that where

Chapter eleven: Heiko Wenig

people literally grew up in a heartbeat of two years; they literally flourished and came into themselves. Did you see much of that?

Heiko: Oh yes. So many people, in a mostly unconscious way, suddenly started to flourish and continued to grow from the decisions they made which were grounded by what they were doing.

To me, that reflects the big circles of life, of learning and development. It isn't just one decision to make. You constantly test and prove your decisions to reinforce them and adjust where necessary. So it wasn't about making one decision and following it, it's a continuous process of decision-making that lays out the path on which people are going through the time, and on which future they go into.

But it's double-bladed, because on the one hand you had to constantly work on it, and on the other there was always the opportunity to change because nothing was solid and it still isn't. So I think it was a great opportunity conscious-wise and in terms of personal growth processes. And when you asked about this interview and its theme of 'thriving through chaos', I thought one of the big things we all have to face is getting more grounded into positivity, making the best of whatever will come. So, lose the illusion that we know what will come and face the truth that nobody really knows what will come, and get really grounded in living that way.

We can get clear on the shallowness of positivity in people who for years have been talking about positive thinking and positive direction. Yet since facing these recent challenges, I've been shocked at how many people who usually provide guidance about the positivity of life went into absolute negativity in a heartbeat. That was really shocking, but it brought up again what is really

Chapter eleven: Heiko Wenig

in the depths of someone when crisis or chaos puts the deepest structures to a test and bring out what's working, what's healthy, what's not and what needs adjusting, healing or grounding.

Many considered themselves positive people, then the chaos tested those deepest structures – their positivity, their purity of life – and whether their power was grounded or not.

Kay: Do you think that outside of the respective fields that you and I work in, people generally don't understand the term 'grounded'?

Heiko: I don't know, but I think so. Even politicians now say, "Okay, I have to be more grounded." I hear that more and more.

Kay: I do too, and since reflecting on your term 'shallowness of positivity' I wonder if there's also a shallowness of grounding.

Heiko: Totally, and to me it's connected

Kay: People talk about it, but maybe don't know how to integrate and ground their experiences. What can you advise people do differently for themselves in terms of grounding?

Heiko: Well in a nutshell, it's about living it. It's very simple and focused to ask yourself the question, "Okay, am I living that or not?" It's an easy decision or an easy question to answer. And then the next question is, "Okay, to which level?" Because no-one is completely grounded in all their life because that's part of the development process to ground more of the good throughout life. So we all live in a constant development of bringing more of the good into life, and these times have put a mirror in front of us to

Chapter eleven: Heiko Wenig

reflect what we really live. So, what is in my consciousness? What are my beliefs? What are my convictions about life, about myself, about society, etc?

Positivity doesn't work by itself until it's grounded in action. This is an example of an illusion that was unveiled and came to the surface during these times.

Kay: I've observed that some people consciously influence their quality of living, while others find it too difficult. It seems to me that some people are becoming more whole, while others are fracturing and splitting away from themselves.

Heiko: Absolutely, and it's completely related to grounding. You look in the mirror and get the reflection, and then you have to decide what to do with it.

Kay: If you look in the mirror, and if you actually deal with what you see …

Heiko: Yes, the thing about that, and what I meant is, this time no-one could look away one way or the other. You had to face it.

Kay: I see in my work a lot of people who look in the mirror and they're devastated because the reflection back is not the reflection they were hoping to project into the mirror. And that wake-up for some people is incredibly painful.

Heiko: But it's a great opportunity to make real changes on every level – the political system, the social system, and definitely personally. All the things we put off time and time again now stare us in the face. The important point is, what all the hard times do is

Chapter eleven: Heiko Wenig

bring your belief and value systems to the surface and to the test.

Kay: I wonder how many people only looked inwardly at their own suffering rather than outwardly at the global situation?

Heiko: Well that's the question. In my experience, it was both. Some look to the bigger picture and others are focused on their own.

Kay: I was thinking about the impact of using the phrase 'hard times' as opposed to 'flowing times.' When we're in hard times, is there something hard physically, metaphorically and metaphysically?
 I'm thinking about the Michelangelo anecdote that he would keep chipping into a rock until the beautiful sculpture within was revealed. Could that be a metaphor for what we're talking about?

Heiko: I like the Michelangelo metaphor, but when it comes to development, the finished thing is still hard, no matter how beautiful; it's still hard.

Kay: Oh, that's interesting and makes sense. One of my big lessons from you over the years is the term 'flow', which you introduced into my consciousness and then into my everyday vocabulary.

Heiko: Really?

Kay: Absolutely, it's a word and a way of being. And yes, you're right, because there is no flow with a hard block in front of it. Well,

Chapter eleven: Heiko Wenig

except a water-eroding flow. Or a molten flow, a lava flow…

Heiko: Oh, all very life-threatening!

Kay: Haha, yes, extreme flow…
So Heiko, you know I think of you as highly evolved human. May I ask, what's your definition of evolution?

Heiko: I've got a very simple view of evolution; to me, it's the manifestation of your life.

Kay: What do you think we can learn from these times so that we can all evolve to manifest our best possible future?

Heiko: We can learn that love and action, compassion in action, bring positivity and light, especially from a meta position. We can learn thousands of things, like how to heal, how to learn about intuitions, trust new ways of going through uncertainty – harmony and balance between solid structures and non-existing structures, and on and on and on.
   There are thousands of things to learn. But again, the way the world learns depends on how much the people are learning. And throughout history I'm disappointed by how much people haven't learned. This time, my feeling is that we definitely have the chance for new, consistent learning.

Kay: I like that, the chance of consistent learning. And some of the words you just used – like intuition, trust, harmony, balance – I also think about how those are words that people use very frequently, and I'm curious about how you would describe their meanings. Say, how would you describe intuition?

Chapter eleven: Heiko Wenig

Heiko: Well, that's a tough question because there are so many definitions of intuition.

Kay: Yes, but yours?

Heiko: Well, that's huge, but in my opinion, intuition is that part of our consciousness that is connected to higher levels of energy like the universe, and which is in the constant flow of information.

Intuition is a certain kind of energy that appears on that field and then hopefully gets through to our conscious or subconscious minds. Some receive it visually and some get it emotionally, but most people associate intuition with a feeling in the gut. To me, that's not intuition, because the gut feeling depends on which other filters you have in place. So not all gut feelings are equally or immediately intuition. But we would have to go into the differences between intuition and wishes, visions and inspiration, to be really clear, which is why I say it's a little bit complicated.

But funnily enough, if we look back at the very beginning of these times, I remember thinking, "Oh, that's another thing that'll

> *"Intuition is that part of our consciousness that is connected to higher levels of energy like the universe, and which is in the constant flow of information...a certain kind of energy"*

Chapter eleven: Heiko Wenig

be over in three months…" I was sloppy about it, I just put it into the box of comparing with previous experience where some kind of pandemic was predicted and then it just disappeared. So I thought, "Ah, that's just another one."

Kay: I thought the same, but I remember chatting with you in Orlando in March 2020, just as the whole world was falling into states of lockdown, and suddenly we realised this was a really serious global problem and we all had to try to find flights home quickly. And I remember you saying that despite this epoch of time being prophesied, you could never comprehend how such a global event could happen, and suddenly you realised it really was happening. And I thought that was remarkable.

Heiko: Absolutely.

Kay: So we've talked a bit about intuition, and I'm now wondering about words like inspiration, insight and intuition; how they can be used interchangeably, and often are, though they clearly mean different things. And with that in mind, I'm still thinking about the title for the book. So at the moment, we're on *Inspirations for Thriving Through Chaos*. But since hearing your perspective on chaos and challenge, I'm wondering about changing the word chaos to challenge.

Heiko: Well, the sound of the title *Thriving Through Chaos* is way more powerful than *Thriving Through Challenges*, I think. I just said I don't think of these times as chaos. The title is pretty good.

Kay: Ah, I see the distinction. Yes, I like the power of the word chaos in the title.

Chapter eleven: Heiko Wenig

Heiko: What I often do for inspiration, especially in recent times, is read or watch biographies and histories of people who went through really hard times, so I can find out what they did and how they did it. And not only hard times. For example, in sports, where athletes go through really hard times before they become successful; the consistency and training to keep going and stay focused. I'm not a sportsman, but looking at is energy-wise or conscious-wise, the mechanisms are always the same. How much effort you put in, how constant your focus is, your motivation is, etc. It's about where the motivation is coming from. I read about climbers who were totally successful and amazing, great record-holders, but the motivations behind the motivations were so different, and that reflected in their way of living in so many ways. And that's interesting for me.

Kay: Can you give an example of what you mean by 'reflected in their way of living'?

Heiko: Yes, some have the motivation to go into extreme situations and say, "If I don't do that, I can't feel myself." Or, "The only way I feel myself is if I constantly challenge myself with life-threatening situations." While others don't need the danger as they've got completely different motivations.

For example, I have one in mind who was driven by the joy of making the impossible possible. That was one of the main goals and motivational points. Of course, he had hard times as well, but all underpinned or flowing on the baseline of joy, while for many others it's just pain-driven. Two rock climbers can appear to have similar behaviours, but their internal processes of thoughts and feelings may be completely different.

What I would say is it's not what you're doing, it's how you're

Chapter eleven: Heiko Wenig

doing it. And to me the distinction is, 'that's more lightful' and 'that's more darkful'. Or, 'that's positive' or 'that's maybe damaging'. And I think these things come to life way more these days. I hope.

To me, in these days, the real question is, "What kind of human do you want to be?"

Kay: I love that question.

Heiko: I ask that of myself often, and very often of other people because, depending on the point of view, it's a very spiritual question, but also a very human and grounding question. I find that in times of struggle, that question can give people a kind of guiding star to orient from or for. And now, especially at this time in which the world is becoming freer again, I think this question becomes even more important.

Kay: I'm thinking about how I would get a client to design their best possible future self as a holographic personal guide. But sometimes that's really difficult for somebody to begin to imagine.

Heiko: Well, absolutely. And to me, the question, "What kind of human do you want to be?" is even higher than that. I think in these times that question becomes more important than ever because of the freedom we have. For example, since so much internet use can now be anonymous, all of a sudden people have the freedom to put out their hate and their rage in extreme and public ways, and it's harder and harder to regulate. I'd ask, "Hey, do you really want to be that person, or a person like that?"

Only 50 years ago, there was a completely different and pretty strict rule set for politeness, for behaviour. And those rules have

Chapter eleven: Heiko Wenig

diluted a lot over the years. We are getting new rules that include new freedoms. So as the outside structures are de-constructing more and more, the freedom of choice expands. So "What kind of human do you want to be?" becomes more and more important.

Kay: Perhaps for some, that's too big a question to contemplate.

Heiko: I don't think so because since childhood I've remembered the quote from Goethe, "Noble be the man, helpful and good." And that became my guiding star of the kind of person I wanted to be. It's not new of course – he wrote that hundreds of years ago.

Kay: Quotes are such a great way to seed something, and so many older and even ancient wisdoms are amazingly accurate and profound for any point in time.

Heiko: Absolutely.

Kay: Heiko, you use the term 'on all levels' very frequently, and you've shared the sort of external levels – the social, economic, political, technological and societal levels. But what about the internal levels of physical, emotional, mental, spiritual?

For example, you were talking about the shallowness of positivity because it can simply be a thought about positivity cycling through the thinking mind, and hasn't yet been processed emotionally and hasn't yet been converted into actions, behaviours. I wonder if that's been part of the wake-up too?

Heiko: Yes, and in the end, the actions show what is there and what is not there. So as you said, if it's just in the mental field and you say, "I'm so positive and see everything positive and I'm full of

Chapter eleven: Heiko Wenig

positivity," but don't act that way, there's a split; the actions reflect where it's not yet completely grounded.

Kay: We've talked a lot from a philosophical perspective of our experiences over the last two years, but what kind of adjustments have you made in your healing energy world?

What about your new decisions, new motivations? Where did you take your inspirations from?

> "I worked through it day by day...it changed and I had to adapt and I got some of the proof of flexibility, which is part of the whole process...I wasn't stopped"

Heiko: Okay, there are so many presuppositions in that question that I can't agree to... I never stop my healing, that's a personal thing. Even talking to people can be very healing-ful. I continued doing healings, as I see it, every day and all that I have talked about today is really what I was doing also for myself, to face where things were not grounded yet and which things I have to live more, and where do I have to make a different decision.

I took all of that continuously on myself and worked through it day by day. And I wasn't completely stopped because it changed and I had to adapt and I got some of the proof of flexibility, which is part of the whole process. I wasn't stopped, and I don't have the feeling that I was on pause.

Chapter eleven: Heiko Wenig

And also you know, I 100% put it on myself to make the very best of things, look at the lightful things in the dark times and nourish them, make them grow and expand in my life.

I overheard a conversation in a flower shop when the first lockdown ended. They were saying, "Hopefully lockdown will continue because I feel so much more relaxed and so much healthier than before. And just thinking of going back to what I did before makes me short of breath and increasing my blood pressure right now." And I think those realisations were reflected in society.

I don't know about you in England, but here in Germany the amount of rubbish thrown away increased dramatically because people tidied up their homes and cleaned up their attics. The rubbish dumps had queues and traffic jams because so many people threw away the rubbish they had found time to sort through. And people started to renovate and make their homes and gardens nicer. So to me, if I look at it energy-wise, it's a reflection of what we were talking about philosophically.

Kay: It's a perfect metaphor, isn't it?

Heiko: Yes, but it wasn't a metaphor, it was real life.

And it showed how people used their time. And how they spent their money on sports equipment, garden stuff, or interior decoration.

Kay: I do think there's a powerful metaphor in there of paying attention to the structures in the home and structures in the mind, and the living structures.

Heiko: And one that's reflected in the other. You know, the benefits of clearing out stuff have been known for many years now.

Kay: Like Marie Kondo, the Japanese lady who specialises in de-cluttering?

Heiko: I think so. That's become a movement and people are thrilled and happy about it. And everybody has the opportunity to clean up and de-clutter on every level; not only on the home level, but also on the soul level, emotional, mental and spiritual level.

Kay: We haven't talked about the soul level.

Heiko: Oh we did, all the time…

Kay: As always, this has been such an enlightening conversation. Before you go, may I ask about your hopes, dreams, desires and aspirations for the next years, for the world?

Heiko: That the decision for the light is lived in the everyday life of everyone and gets rooted even more.

Kay: Perfect! That's a wonderful phrase to end this chapter, and this book.

Heiko: Is it? For me it's just the beginning…

www.heikowenig.com

AFTERWORD

Bearing in mind you're reading this, I'm assuming you've delved into some of the preceding 250 or so pages (or are you one of those back-to-front readers? If so, welcome to my world…).

Whether you've already thoroughly digested this book or simply picked it up out of curiosity, I wonder what chimes with you? Is it the story of a man whose tough childhood and a dark night of the soul inspire the flow philosophy he lives by today? Perhaps it's the vision of one of the great teachers, thinkers and innovators whose insights within these pages are infused with gifts for any and every mind.

What really matters is that there is something for everyone in this collection. It has been my great privilege to compile and edit it, in the process re-discovering the interviews my friend and teacher Kay Cooke conducted with inspirational figures. Their philosophies for thriving through and beyond the chaos of our fast-changing world are deeply inspiring and enriching. I believe it is our responsibility to share their wisdom as widely as possible, particularly among our young people.

As a writer and editor, the considered use of language with clarity of purpose is at the heart of all I do. In recent years, I have edited works by leading thinkers including Dr Richard Bandler, Owen Fitzpatrick, Kate Benson, and Kay Cooke, each revealing the magic in words for guiding us all in venturing beyond our limitations. This book continues that journey.

As I leave you to continue to read and re-read these conversations, I share with you a life philosophy which most resonates with me in these pages. This is courtesy of the artist Alexander Miller, who says: "I've found that the more you surrender yourself to life and stop kicking and pushing and shoving and forcing, life kind of carries you. It's like a gentle breeze; it floats you along and it'll take you where you're meant to be."

Jane Pikett
Editor
February 2022

THANK YOU

Handling other people's words is an honour which carries with it great responsibility. The process from initial transcription through to final edit is demanding and I'd like to thank David Cooke, Thomas Allinson, and Sophie Cooper for their part in the initial transcriptions of these conversations.

I'm eternally grateful for the ongoing guidance, words work, and perspective of my trusted colleague, editor and friend Jane Pikett (www.the-editor.pro).

www.ingramcontent.com/pod-product-compliance
Lightning Source LLC
Chambersburg PA
CBHW041305110526
44590CB00028B/4253